# Multicultural Education:

## Commitments, Issues, and Applications

# Multicultural Education:

## Commitments, Issues, and Applications

Prepared by
The ASCD Multicultural Education Commission

Edited by Carl A. Grant

Association for Supervision
and Curriculum Development
1701 K Street, N.W., Suite 1100
Washington, D.C. 20006

Stock number: 611-77108

Library of Congress Catalog Card Number: 77-080575

ISBN 0-87120-084-8

# Contents

# Foreword

This booklet is the product of ASCD's Multicultural Commission. Beginning with a position statement on multicultural education, the document reflects varying views of a complex concept.

James B. Macdonald, in "Democracy in Education: Cultural Pluralism," suggests that schooling, in order to be an effective educational force in a democratic society, must choose the option of "developing human potential, increasing participation, and opting for pluralism." He examines and rejects standard approaches to multicultural education as directly acceptant of a dominant school culture. Meaningful multicultural education encompasses the school as a "living laboratory" where multiethnic encounters are a part of the "unstudied curriculum."

Michael W. Apple addresses another aspect of multicultural education in his paper entitled "Justice as a Curricular Concern: Legal Mechanisms and Student Rights." Apple points out that much school activity is harmful rather than helpful to children who are culturally different; consequently, our schools are basically unjust to a significant portion of their clientele. He challenges curriculum workers to examine what happens in schools with a view to becoming advocates for students and for guaranteeing rights to students who are most often denied them, especially minority students. The paper focuses on the law as a tool which may be used to challenge many school actions which deny rights and justice to students.

Carl A. Grant examines the relationship between anthropology and education that is multicultural. He illustrates how the principles of anthropology can help educators understand the impact of culture on the school and can clarify their perceptions of the role of the school culture in shaping the lives of children.

Susan L. Melnick examines sexism in the English language and presents alternatives which have implications for schooling and for society in general.

Geneva Gay, Muriel Saville-Troike, H. Prentice Baptiste, Jr., Gloria Grant, Mirian Ortiz and Lourdes Travieso discuss the specifics of curriculum design and multicultural materials and instructional activities.

Carol Dodge discusses the stereotypic portrayal of the American Indian and suggests guidelines and topics for the development of curriculum materials and classroom activities which portray contemporary American Indian life honestly and accurately.

Papers by Florence Yoshiwara, Allen Schmieder and Mary F. Crum illuminate the international dimension of cultural pluralism and Kaoru Yamamoto points out the need for research which will be of help in developing education that is multicultural.

The booklet is an excellent resource for curriculum workers, teachers, administrators and researchers. It is a significant indication of ASCD's commitment to cultural pluralism as reflected in its projects and in its publications.

ELIZABETH S. RANDOLPH, *President, 1977-78*
*Association for Supervision*
*and Curriculum Development*

# Introduction

Multicultural education is more than merely one important idea in the educational galaxy; it is a living, growing, changing concept, responding to a living, growing, changing world. Or as the ASCD Statement on Multicultural Education phrases it, "Multicultural education is a continuous, systematic process that will broaden and diversify as it develops." Equally important, however, is the content of multicultural education, the core of which is respect for all people, regardless of their differences — in fact, the recognition and prizing of diversity.

This book — *Multicultural Education: Commitments, Issues, and Applications* — is an outgrowth of the work of ASCD's Multicultural Commission. As chairperson of this commission, I have had the honor of being the principal organizer of this project.

The viewpoints and backgrounds of the authors of the articles in this book are diverse — and deliberately so, for this book should itself demonstrate the awareness of cultural pluralism that is a basis for multicultural education. As a result, each author tends to have a definition of multicultural education that varies somewhat from that of his/her fellow authors. All, however, have in common the fact that they are committed to affirming diversity — both in people and in languages. All the authors are emphasizing respect for all people.

*Multicultural Education: Commitments, Issues, and Applications* has attempted to cover all three of the areas mentioned in its title. However, in preparing this book, it has become clear that commitments and issues abound, but there is less material available in the area of application. This book includes four brief examples of applications which I believe are illustrative of the kinds of activities that can and should be developed in order to implement multicultural education in any setting, mono- or multicultural. I hope that others will continue to work in this area, as well as in the areas of commitments and issues.

Implementation of multicultural education is vital at this point in our history. All our aspirations toward improvement of education for *all* children are tied to the success of multicultural education. Multicultural education is a tool for elimination of divisive forms of discrimination with regard to race, sex, class, age, physical size, and handicaps.

## ACKNOWLEDGMENTS

The editor wishes to acknowledge his appreciation and indebtedness to several persons who assisted in completing this book: Gwen Woolever and Rita Johnson, who exercised patience and understanding while typing the manuscript; Susan Clifford, who rendered valuable assistance in editing the classroom activities; Nadine Goff, for her valuable assistance in copy editing and proofing the manuscripts; and, last but not least, all the members of the Multicultural Commission, past and present, for their support.

# 1

# Encouraging Multicultural Education

The ASCD Multicultural Education Commission

ASCD's commitment to multicultural education emanates from the realities of life in the United States. It also emerges from the Association's consistent affirmation of democratic processes and humanistic ideals.

We live in a culturally pluralistic society. With the increasing complexity and interdependence of economic, political, and social affairs, similarities and differences among cultural groups become more pronounced. A single national culture is no longer acceptable as a feasible concept for educational processes and interpersonal behavior. A dynamic realignment of political and economic power among various interest groups in our country and among world nations emphasizes the need for increased understanding of ourselves and others.

Attempts to understand "other" people and bases for "others'" decisions, intentions, and values must be broadened beyond historically monocultural perspectives. Shifting balances of power reduce abilities of adherents of the dominant culture to control their own destinies, as well as those of "others." This fact certainly necessitates a deeper reexamination of "others" if we are to understand and coexist with them. Life in a culturally pluralistic society requires fundamental changes in educational philosophies, processes, and practices. We might consider these as basic needs for human renewal.

An initial step toward human renewal must emphasize that many different cultures exist in the United States. It must also include a recognition of their right to exist, and an acceptance of the fact that they represent humanity's potential in a very altruistic sense.

1

Human renewal must further recognize the validity and viability of cultural diversity. As educators, we must strive to understand cultural pluralism and develop an empathy for more than the obvious "trappings" that might characterize a culture. It is therefore time to translate our concern for individual development into the more difficult task of understanding individuals within the context of their cultural group experiences.

As we accept the realities of cultural pluralism, a growing recognition of the worth, dignity, and integrity of each individual becomes defined in behavior — in the cultural context of each individual. Thus, our concern for maximizing individual development of human potential must increasingly be viewed as a continually emerging and evolving one, shaped by different cultural contexts, which nourish the growth and development of the individual. There is no single criterion of human potential applicable to all. Instead, complex and varied sets of coherent values, motives, attitudes, and attributes — which determine behavior patterns — exist among cultural groups. Added to this is the effect of economic, political, and social racism toward nonwhite minority groups. All of these factors must be considered in our efforts to design opportunities for educational experiences that will maximize human dignity and potential for all individual students.

Different cultural and social environments have determining influences on individual perception and behavior. Two such environments are our early-life experiences and our technological society. The earliest associations of a child form the basis of his/her cultural heritage. Cultural heritage is the essence of relationship patterns, linguistic and expressive communication, and the fundamental values and attitudes through which each child grows. To ignore, or invalidate this living experience for any individual is, in effect, to distort and diminish the possibilities for developing that person's potential.

The growing impact of the complexity of life in our highly technological and industrialized society necessitates recognition of cultural pluralism, and should foster active efforts for its positive perpetuation. We are all in danger of being alienated, bureaucratized, and depersonalized by the rationality of the ethos of industrial technology. Not only are ethnic minorities being deculturalized and dehumanized, but *all* of us are being sized and fitted to sets of specifications that are essentially depersonalizing and destructive to human individuality. In a very real sense, members of the majority culture or dominant segment of society are just as invalidated as *individuals* as are members of minority groups and cultures. All face the superstructure of technological-industrial-economic rationality. Cultural pluralism emerges not only as a social fact, but also as a positive ideal to preserve the integrity of all individuals. It is necessary for the development of a more humane society through democratic processes.

## Definition

ASCD's commitment to cultural pluralism evolves from a concern for more valid educational futures, and a realization of the social and cultural changes taking place in our society. Cultural pluralism is neither the traditionalist's separatism nor the assimilationist's melting pot. It is a composite that recognizes the uniqueness and value of every culture. Cultural pluralism acknowledges that no group lives in isolation, but that, instead, each group influences and is influenced by others.

In educational terms, the recognition of cultural pluralism has been labeled "multicultural education." The essential goals of multicultural education embrace: (a) recognizing and prizing diversity; (b) developing greater understanding of other cultural patterns; (c) respecting individuals of all cultures; and (d) developing positive and productive interaction among people *and* among experiences of diverse cultural groups.

Multicultural education, as interpreted by ASCD, is a humanistic concept based on the strength of diversity, human rights, social justice, and alternative life choices for all people. It is mandatory for quality education. It includes curricular, instructional, administrative, and environmental efforts to help students avail themselves of as many models, alternatives, and opportunities as possible from the full spectrum of our cultures. This education permits individual development in any culture. Each individual simultaneously becomes aware that every group (ethnic, cultural, social, and racial) exists autonomously as a part of an interrelated and interdependent societal whole. Thus, the individual is encouraged to develop social skills that will enable movement among and cooperation with other cultural communities and groups.

Multicultural education is a continuous, systematic process that will broaden and diversify as it develops. It views a culturally pluralistic society as a positive force that welcomes differences as vehicles for understanding. It includes programs that are systematic in nature; that enhance and preserve cultural distinctions, diversities, and similarities; and that provide individuals with a wide variety of options and alternatives.

Multicultural education goes beyond an understanding and acceptance of different cultures. It recognizes the right of different cultures to exist, as separate and distinct entities, and acknowledges their contribution to the societal entity. It evolves from fundamental understandings of the interaction of divergent cultures *within* the culture of the United States. If multicultural education is to achieve its goals, the concepts that constitute its foundations must pervade the educational experiences of *all* students.

The concepts of multicultural education seem rather familiar — and they are. What is new is contextual in nature, a sifting and winnowing to understand these goals in cultural terms. What previously seemed appropriate goals in terms of *individuals* now gain in perspective by looking at individuals in the context of cultural realities (including both origins and experiences).

The major application factor for multicultural education concerns the quality of the interaction — that which characterizes content and context of the school in relation to each child's unique cultural group reality. The critical commitment must be to *diversification*, since without this acceptance and its deliberate advancement, there is little hope of building greater understanding or greater respect for individuals. Therefore, the heart of multicultural education pertains to the interactional dimensions of human behavior, and the development of effective skills to facilitate such functioning. Multicultural education can be addressed by the type of interaction that is encouraged and structured in the schools' curricula and environment. It includes the broadest range of potential human interaction, both in content and context.

Multicultural education emphasizes the development of communication skills to enable cross-cultural and inter-ethnic group interaction. It endorses the development of perceptual, analytical, and application skills, which can be applied in both formal and informal, personal and institutional settings. It also places a high priority on developing abilities to make dependable, responsible decisions, and to gain, maintain, and exercise political power. The concern for multicultural education is fundamentally a concern for maximizing individual ability — to use communicative and interactional skills to improve the quality of life in a culturally pluralistic, multiracial, and highly technological society.

## Application

In practical terms, ASCD's application of multicultural education calls for an examination of educational content and processes. ASCD's goals include the creation and advancement of understanding, along with a respect for differences that can lead to an altruistic development of human potential. A number of suggestions are apparent at both content and process levels. The following suggestions are clearly illustrative and are not intended to be comprehensive:

1. Examine text materials for evidence of racism, classism, sexism, and realistic treatment of cultural pluralism in American society.

2. Develop new curricula for all levels of schooling — curricula that enhance and promote cultural diversity.

3. Provide opportunities to learn about and interact with a variety of ethnic groups and cultural experiences.

4. Include the study of concepts from the humanistic and behavioral sciences, which are applicable for understanding human behavior.

5. Organize curricula around universal human concerns, which transcend usual subject-matter disciplines; bring multicultural perspectives to bear in the study of such issues.

6. Broaden the kinds of inquiry used in the school to incorporate and facilitate the learning of more humanistic modes of inquiry.

7. Create school environments that radiate cultural diversity.

8. Maximize the school as a multicultural setting, with the idea of utilizing the positive contributions of all groups to accomplish common tasks and not just to reduce deficiencies for the deprived.

9. Recognize and utilize bilingualism as a positive contribution to the communication process, and include bilingual programs of instruction for monolingual children.

10. Examine rules, norms, and procedures of students and staff with the purpose of facilitating the development of learning strategies and techniques that do not penalize and stigmatize diversity, but rather, encourage and prize it.

11. Institute a system of shared governance in the schools, in which all groups can enter equally in the learning and practice of democratic procedures.

12. Organize time, space, personnel, and resources to facilitate the maximum probability and flexibility of alternative experiences for all youngsters.

13. Institute staffing patterns (involving both instructional and non-instructional positions) that reflect our culturally pluralistic and multiracial society.

14. Design and implement preservice and in-service programs to improve staff ability to successfully implement multicultural education.

ASCD is committed to the mandates of multicultural education. The Association endorses the reality of cultural pluralism, as well as the potential for the advancement of human life through the acceptance and prizing of diversity, which makes possible greater understanding among groups, with respect for individuals. It recognizes that specific and concrete commitments must be an integral part of all ASCD's activities, *and* of the entire educational enterprise, if we are to more effectively advance the cause of social functioning and educational proficiency for our diverse population.

# 2
# Living Democratically in Schools: Cultural Pluralism

James B. Macdonald

The movement toward multicultural education arises from the practical reality of the failure of assimilation of subcultures into the historically dominant culture of American life. We do, in fact, remain a pluralistic society. This reality has been ignited in recent times by our awareness of minority groups striving for social equity and justice via civil rights movements and other forms of liberating pressures.

Analysis of the schools and how they function, especially with more recent concerns about output variables, has raised serious questions that do not yet lead to comfortable answers for educators. How does one explain the differences in performance of youngsters representing varying minority, religious, social class, racial, and sex groupings?

The answers do not "fall out" easily although there is no dearth of hypotheses. We, most of us, had naively assumed that providing equal facilities with equal access to the dominant culture was primarily what was needed. We have little evidence, even where these have been successfully embodied in school programs, that the outcomes are reasonably equitable.

It is now eminently clear that schools and school goals are directly affected by the family background and the broader social structure and uses of schooling. As in most other aspects of life we are now aware of the social ecology, the interrelationship of all our social institutions, reflected in this case in schooling. This is simply to say, in old-fashioned terms, that education is not synonymous with schooling. What we really have gained lately is a much more sophisticated set of data to document this truism.

What this, in effect, means is that equal access and equal facilities in school programs can never hope to solve the problems of equal access to the "good" life for a large number of youngsters in our society. The good life is, of course, defined by the patterns of success that have evolved through the dominant culture in the context of our industrialized urban society. The critical variables from a dominant cultural viewpoint would seem to be the need for standardization of cultural experience in the family lives of children, and a complete acceptance of the status quo in our social structures, if subcultural groups are to enter fully into success patterns.

Problems and conflict immediately arise with these suggestions. There is little agreement that cultural values, norms, and behavior patterns learned in the home in the dominant culture represent the best attributes of human beings. What was once so easily dismissed as cultural deprivation now is seen more lucidly as cultural difference. Further, there is no assurance that the present social structures, characterized by technology, bureaucracy, and a consumer citizen's role, are the epitome of the good life. In fact, one would suppose that in a democratic society social structures would continue to evolve toward more and more humane conditions.

The options before us would appear to boil down to three:

1. Leave things alone.
2. Impose greater control over the lives of individuals.
3. Accept and facilitate differences in a non-punitive manner.

The first, I suggest, is untenable if for no other reason than that minority groups will not settle for this. Between the second and third the only viable way to proceed in the spirit of our democratic ideals would appear to be the option of developing human potential, increasing participation, and opting for pluralism. In this sense we must face up to the acceptance of multicultural schooling.

## Multicultural Schooling

The advocates of multicultural schooling have proposed many courses of action. One such proposal is multiethnic studies (begun primarily by the black studies movement). Another thrust has come under the aegis of local control, a return to separatism and segregation in many cases. Still a third is based in developing greater understanding of children from various backgrounds so that they/we may learn how to "motivate" them to accept and achieve in the standard curriculum.

To my way of thinking, none of these definitions is satisfactory, although there may be circumstances in which they are positive and desirable. Each, in its own way, is directly acceptant of a dominant school culture. To me, the promise of multicultural education rests in the enlargement of human potential by the actual living in multicultural situations in classrooms. Thus, it seems to me that education has as its basic meaning the process of helping each person transcend the parochialism of his/her own time and place, and the creation and fostering of human possibilities that may be entered into and eventually chosen as the most fulfilling personal values and life styles.

Thus, what multicultural education means to me is the recognition of each person in the context of his/her cultural background. In this sense the individual is not abstracted from a living context and placed upon the gridwork of standardized norms. Further, the recognition of the power of a cultural upbringing demands the acceptance of the real worth of the context from which a person comes as a self-confident stepping off place for personal development.

## Culture

The critical need in multicultural education is a clarification of what we mean by culture, for we really will have very little opportunity to distinguish meaningful activity in schools if we are not clear about the term. This is not an easy task, since there is really not a clearly accepted agreement among social scientists.

On the broadest level culture tends to be related to or defined as the symbolic universe of a group of persons. In this sense it refers to the meanings people attach to relationships to self and others, to humankind's extensions, for example, tools, technology, etc., to institutions, ideas, and other groups of people, and to each human's relations to cosmic circumstances.

This leaves all areas of the school curriculum within the definition of culture. However, it seems to me that the cultural heritage as the course of study is perhaps the least important from a cultural analysis point of view in terms of the multicultural education movement.

Rather, I suggest that, for example, Edward T. Hall's concern is of more import and value for viewing school activity from a multicultural perspective. From Hall's viewpoint, the so-called cultural heritage, that is, the body of cultural knowledge and skills, may be the very danger that must be transcended. As Hall states:

I would suggest another alternative, namely that once man began evolving his extensions, particularly language, tools, institutions, he got caught in a web of what I term extension transference and was both alienated from himself and incapable of controlling the monsters he had created. In this sense, he was advanced at the expense of that part of himself that he has extended, and as a consequence has ended up by regressing his nature in its many forms. Man's goal from here on out should be to rediscover that self.[1]

What seems to me to be infinitely more important than the course of study of schooling is the quality of everyday life in the schools. Excluding the practical reason that there appears to me no way we can construct totally different courses of study for each subcultural group to be operational simultaneously, the real impact and promise of cultural diversity appears in, as Berger says "the web of meanings that allow the individual to navigate his way through the ordinary events and encounters of his life with others."[2]

The assumption here is that the traditional dominant cultural course of study, its programming and sequencing, are completely arbitrary. This shared technological-consumer knowledge and skill can be learned at any time and in a variety of places given the willingness of an educative society to provide the access. What is infinitely more important is the self-concept we hold of ourselves and the potential for our human possibilities by the encounter of cultural differences in our everyday lives. In mundane terms, an analogy may be made to the learning of a foreign language. If we wish to learn it well and experience the culture and its impact on us for our development as human beings, it is far better to go live in a foreign country than to sit in a booth with earphones at any high school. What focusing on the everyday life of youngsters in our schools in multicultural setting does is to provide the same kind of living laboratory. Quite frankly, I think it is the only really meaningful embodiment of multicultural education in schools. The precedent for looking at schools in this manner is already with us in the concern for the hidden curriculum,[3] or the unstudied curriculum,[4] or life in the classrooms, [5] or the everyday quality of classroom living.[6]

[1]Edward T. Hall. *Beyond Culture*. Garden City, New York: Doubleday & Company, Inc., 1976. Copyright © 1976 by Edward T. Hall. Reprinted by permission of Doubleday & Company, Inc. See also, by the same author: *The Silent Language*. Garden City, New York: Doubleday & Company, Inc., 1959; *The Hidden Dimension*. Garden City, New York: Doubleday & Company, Inc., 1966.

[2]Peter Berger, Bridgette Berger, and Hansfried Kellner. *The Homeless Mind: Modernization and Consciousness*. New York: Random House, Inc., 1973.

[3]Michael Apple. "The Hidden Curriculum and the Nature of Conflict." *Interchange* 2 (4); 1971.

[4]Norman Overly, editor. *The Unstudied Curriculum. Its Impact on Children*. Washington, D.C.: Association for Supervision and Curriculum Development, 1970. p. 127.

[5]Philip Jackson. *Life in Classrooms*. New York: Holt, Rinehart & Winston, 1968.

[6]James B. Macdonald. "The Quality of Everyday Life in School." James B. Macdonald and Esther Zaret, editors. *Schools in Search of Meaning*. Washington, D.C.: Association for Supervision and Curriculum Development, 1975.

## Dimensions of Living Culture in Schools

Given these premises, assumptions, and opinions it would make sense to examine more critically the dimensions of cultural activity and the multicultural implications of such activity.

What this in effect means is that multicultural education must be conceptualized and organized in terms of the daily lives of students. Further, it will be of little value simply to place students from diverse cultures together and hope that by some process of osmosis learnings will be picked up. Nor does it mean that we should didactically teach multiple cultures as the ideational beliefs of diverse groups. Each of these options, it seems to me, is bracketed by a standard culture which encapsulates and overpowers the multicultural intentions.

One avenue that is worth trying comes from an exploration of the idea of culture. Culture has often tended to mean differences, so that multicultural education becomes education for many different groups of youngsters. It is at least worth asking whether the key to such educational efforts may lie in a more careful analysis of the knowledge we possess about the dimensions of culture.

Here, again, it is important to note that the cultural "media is the message," not the linguistic content of messages. Thus, as Edward T. Hall has argued, it is the hidden dimensions of culture that make the greater impact. These are primarily nonverbal and are the structural glue which organizes our activity and directly impact upon our self-concepts and visions of our possibilities. It is in these aspects of culture, rather than the products of culture, such as art, religion, philosophy, and language, that I would look for leads to creating viable multicultural education programs.

Hall identified ten interrelated and dynamic non-verbal systems of culture. They are, again, structural ways of organizing human activity that are normally hidden from us. These ten systems are: (a) interaction, (b) materials, (c) associations, (d) defense, (e) work, (f) play, (g) bisexuality, (h) learning, (i) space, and (j) time.

What these subsystems represent in school terms are ways of organizing or structuring the human activity regardless of the subject matter content of the program; and as such in our traditional and standardized educational system are reflections of the dominant culture, variously called "Anglo" or "white middle class" or "Western European urban," etc. It is this "structure" which most clearly relates to the sense of the quality of living in schools and most directly to the emotional/attitudinal/motivational/self-concept nexus of the schools.

**Reflecting Upon Cultural Subsystems in Schooling**

When we think about the implications of this school culture it reveals a number of familiar awarenesses, some not so familiar, and all in a somewhat different perspective which may prove more useful than earlier ones.

In schooling terms these cultural subsystems are interrelated (as in any cultural setting). Thus *work*, for example, is distinguished from *play* and given priority over play in the serious business of the school. The serious business refers to using *time* in a serial nature (one thing at a time, that is, work activity), in a specific *space*, and with movement in space carefully prescribed. Materials are also work-appropriate and to be used in prescribed ways for work tasks. Interaction and associations, that is, the process of approved communication and the groupings of people, are also work specific, prescribed, and supposedly facilitative. Sexuality is carefully repressed on the one hand, but utilized in its bisexual implication for many management facilitative tasks such as lining up (boys and girls). Learning is the outcome of working, but also it is embedded in time, place, interaction, association, material, bisexuality, and play. One learns in school, under appropriate prescribed procedures, by doing work (not playing) in facilitative interactions and associations, with identified relevant materials in specific spaces under carefully controlled time sequences.

The standard procedures, structures, and organizational patterns are well known from our own observation and experience. It is proposed here that the cultural subsystems and the standard non-verbal patterns are dominant culture specific. In this sense they provide a tacit cultural dimension which is more or less at odds or alien to the tacit organization of non-verbal culture for a great many (probably the majority) of youngsters in the American schools.

This realization, of the tacit subcultural dimension, helps explain one of the major problems with special programs for culturally "deprived" or "different" youngsters. The emphasis has seldom been placed upon examining the non-verbal or tacit cultural patterns that are built into the work (school) situation. It is really very little wonder that culturally different youngsters, that is, from the dominant culture, cannot overcome their own non-verbal cultural conditioning and compete equally in a different non-verbal cultural pattern. The possibility of doing so would, of course, vary with different subcultural groups (as it does).

In this light cultural pluralism or multiethnic education (as discussed here) becomes one of the main schooling possibilities for providing equal access to the overt and symbolic substance of the total culture.

## Culturally Pluralistic Programs

We are immediately faced with a plethora of problems when considering what culturally pluralistic programs would look like. It is necessary, in other words, to identify the basic structure(s) of schooling that would facilitate pluralism. It should be clear that pluralism has little meaning outside the context of comparison and that any attempt to escape structure is an illusory one. Freedom, whether it be personal or cultural, is always within boundaries.

Here I would agree with Gibson Winter[7] that acceptance of *pluralism* necessitates commitment to the goals of human *liberation*, and the social processes of equal *participation*. In less lofty terms (and more educationally comfortable ones), this means that programs designed to facilitate human development in culturally pluralistic contexts must be committed to the development of individual potential through the cultural nexus of the specific individuals and by utilizing democratic processes which allow for full participation of the persons in schools in making decisions which determine the quality of their experiences. In even more mundane terms, there is no substitute for the acceptance of each person for what he/she is and could become; and, legitimizing this acceptance through the process of full participation in the determination of activity.

One of the most promising directions for realizing the above ideals would appear to be making the latent cultural subsystems mentioned earlier (time, space, etc.) manifest to the persons involved (bringing them to verbal awareness) and then making the subcultural systems negotiable by deliberation and reflection on the part of all concerned. This would indeed be a "tall order" for most schools. Yet, it seems hypocritical to foster concerns for cultural pluralism without going to what is premised here to be the heart of the matter.

The implications of this approach suggest that a much greater concern for "coming to know" each other and for entering into negotiation through planning and deliberation are basic cornerstones. Beyond this the making and remaking of the patterns of structure for school activity would be a continual process.

The learning environment (or curriculum) takes on special meaning here. That is, cultural pluralism will demand a much broader and more flexible kind of encounter for the people involved. The program will by necessity need to be based in each classroom with adults, but evolve out of these settings into the community at large, interdisciplinary study themes, and special interest centers.

[7]Gibson Winter. *Being Free*. New York: Macmillan, 1970.

Probably the most critical problem will reside in what is usually called the definition of objectives. It should be clear that if learning expectations are defined purely in terms of traditional school goals, then pluralism will continually collapse into rigid, dominant cultural orientation, since the standard expectations of the school already are embodied in this culture. What will be needed are goals which transcend these limitations and provide a more universal orientation to the schools.

In place of the usual cognitive, affective, and skill objectives, goal statements will need to deal with some qualities such as "life values" — values in the sense that they represent the integration of cognitive, affective, and action components of culture into meaning and behaviors which are meaningful in the total life (not just school) of the learner. In other words, learning will need to be redefined to focus upon value as coming to know through cognitive awareness, emotionally positive affect, and commitment to action as behavioral wholes and not separate aspects of behavior.

In summary then, one projected program format for cultural pluralism concerns redefining goals in broad holistic terms; providing an environment which allows for activity in the community, in interdisciplinary study, with special interest and need centers; and with full participation in the school community, all evolving out of the close personal relationships with knowledgeable, helping adults.

**Final Note**

There is no need to concern ourselves about multiethnic education in the context of cultural pluralism if we are not committed to a democratic society. If we are committed to democracy then there is no alternative but to respect the individual in his/her cultural difference and provide for each person's development through his/her own life history and unique characteristics.

Programs based upon cultural pluralism are affirmative action programs, not simply programs which affirm the rights of individuals in the context of structures which predispose the competitive success of certain subcultural groups. Further, the dignity of the person, as Gabriel Marcel points out,[8] is not best represented by either the concept of *liberty* or *equality*, but rather by commitment to *fraternity*. Liberty, per se, leads to domination by subcultural "privileged" groups. Equality is meaningless beyond abstractions in a society composed of differing subcultural groups. It is concern for each as a brother-sister that provides the cornerstone of real democracy for a program built upon cultural pluralism.

---

[8]Gabriel Marcel. *The Existential Background of Human Dignity*. Cambridge, Massachusetts: Harvard University Press, 1963.

# 3

# Justice as a Curricular Concern: Legal Mechanisms and Student Rights

Michael W. Apple

## Justice and Educational Design

"Are schools just?" is a question many educators do not think to ask. Because of the efficiency (some might call it factory) model which dominates the field of curriculum and because of the conservative ideological and economic roots on which the field rests, concepts such as justice seem somewhat out of place in curricular and more general educational argumentation. Yet, as a field that often seeks to influence concretely the lives of students, the lack of an overt commitment to justice and to the quality of life in institutions of schooling should be a major concern of us all. If we accept the role of mere technicians then I can stop here. But I think that none among us would accept even for a moment such a definition of self. For as an activity of influence, curriculum design — designing of educational environments — must be held accountable to notions such as justice and ethical responsibility in one's conduct with others if its members are to be more than experts for hire by existing and often problematic institutions.

Much of my previous work has centered around examining the conservative ideologies which guide a good deal of curricular thought and practice, and on the mechanisms within schools which embody these ideological rules: for example, the selection and organization of ideological knowledge in schools (what has come to be called the hidden curriculum), the modes of evaluation school people employ to define political and educational problems

14

out of existence, and the labeling process that stems from these modes of valuing and which acts as a form of social control in schools.[1] I have argued that these ideological rules make it difficult for educators to deal with the economic, ethical, and political complexities that confront anyone concerned with getting beneath the surface rhetoric surrounding the process of schooling. In short, we have continually shied away from asking serious questions about the nexus of economic and political power that lies behind much that goes on in schools. In so doing we have neglected our own personal responsibility in illuminating this problem. Such a responsibility is even more critically important when one considers the topic of multicultural education. As I have pointed out, a good deal of the everyday activity in schools ultimately results in actually hurting not helping children who are culturally distinct or "different."[2] Because of this, it is possible to argue that our educational institutions are basically unjust to a significant portion of their clientele. Part of this problem is the result of the lack of legal rights, and the power which results from these constitutionally guaranteed rights, for students in schools.

Since one of the curriculum field's concerns is and must be the question of the power to control what does and does not happen within the school, then part of our task should be an *in depth* examination of fields whose fundamental roles are that of dealing with the provision of checks on power within and among our institutions. Just as Mann, for instance, asks us to focus on the economic forces surrounding the school from a critical perspective because of the fundamental question of who controls the dominant institutions of this society,[3] so too must we look to legal precedents to complement that focus. For it seems to me that advocacy requires a certain degree of sophistication. One area in which curriculum scholarship is sorely lacking this sophistication is that of legal expertise. This is especially important for those curriculum workers and other educators like myself who are committed to both the student rights movement and to guaranteeing rights to those students who are most often denied them, especially "minority" students. All too often, legal "weapons" are considered the province of administrators, with the unfortunate result of having the law act as a repressive instrument

---

[1]See, for example: Michael W. Apple. "The Hidden Curriculum and the Nature of Conflict." *Interchange* 2 (4): 29-41; 1971; "The Process and Ideology of Valuing in Educational Settings." Michael W. Apple, Michael Subkoviak, and Henry Lufler, Jr., editors. *Educational Evaluation: Analysis and Responsibility.* Berkeley: McCutchan, 1974. pp. 3-34; and Michael W. Apple. "Commonsense Categories and Curriculum Thought." James B. Macdonald and Esther Zaret, editors. *Schools in Search of Meaning.* Washington, D.C.: Association for Supervision and Curriculum Development, 1975. pp. 116-48.

[2]Apple, "Commonsense Categories and Curriculum Thought," *op. cit.*

[3]John S. Mann. "On Contradictions in Schools." James B. Macdonald and Esther Zaret, editors. *Schools in Search of Meaning.* Washington, D.C.: Association for Supervision and Curriculum Development, 1975. pp. 95-115.

rather than as a useful tool for requiring greater responsiveness by public institutions. In this paper, I would like to focus on the law as such an instrument, one that, when combined with other political, economic, and educational resources and used by the more progressive forces in this society, can be employed as a means of challenging many of the unquestioned actions taken by school people that deny rights and justice to students, particularly students who are black, Latino, or otherwise culturally distinct.

At the outset, let me point to an important fact. We should realize that just because it is the law there is no guarantee that democratic rights will be respected within the institutions of schooling. In fact, extended observations in schools over the past few years have led me to conclude that there is widespread disregard for students' and teachers' civil rights. Furthermore, there seems to be extreme discomfort over the topic itself.[4]

For example, a little-known "incident" documents the controversy and often outright fear raised by the act of merely teaching students their rights in schools. The March 19, 1973, issue of the *Scholastic News Citizen*, a publication of Scholastic Magazines was devoted to the topic of student rights. Under the title of "Have You Got Rights?" it gave students information on a number of rights issues, in language a student could easily understand and in a relatively "neutral" way. By neutral I mean that it told students the concrete rights many students *did* already have and also asked them to be sensible about how they used them. Among the specific questions treated by the colorful pamphlet were hair and dress codes, pledging the flag, locker and desk searches, censorship in the putting out of school newspapers, freedom of assembly, right to petition (to "ask" as they put it), punishment, and being "kicked out of school."

Apparently, a negative response by teachers and administrators to even treating student rights in a publication aimed at the students themselves was so vociferous that less than two weeks later on March 30, 1973, the publisher of Scholastic Magazines sent out a letter to all of the subscribers of *Scholastic News Citizen* that apologized for the manner in which the publication had dealt with the topic of student rights. The publisher sought to counterbalance this situation by promising to publish an article on "student responsibilities" in an upcoming issue and promised greater "vigilance" in the future. Thus, it seems even giving information to the people who hold rights legally in the first place can be a controversial act. Sometimes the mere act of honesty is apt to create problems.

---

[4]Cf.: Michael W. Apple and Thomas Brady. "Towards Increasing the Potency of Student Rights Claims." Vernon Haubrich and Michael W. Apple, editors. *Schooling and the Rights of Children*. Berkeley: McCutchan and the National Society for the Study of Education, 1975. pp. 198-207.

Now I must admit not to be surprised by the reaction of the schools or by the response to this reaction by the publisher. We have a rather long history of supporting the extension of constitutional guarantees in the abstract and being less than overjoyed when they are indeed practiced by people who are usually disenfranchised or oppressed. This can serve as a potent reminder that legalistic approaches to the problem of the lack of responsiveness of our institutions are and can only be partial solutions. In fact, because of the emerging economic crisis of advanced industrial societies and the slowing of many of the forces behind the student rights movement — anti-war protests, the civil rights struggle, the near demise of the New Left — there can be a significant erosion in the gains made by parents, students, rights advocates, minority groups, and others in their struggle to expand the constitutional guarantees of children in schools.

One other point needs to be made, I think. It is important to see the problem of students' rights to their own history, culture, and traditions in the larger setting of rights in general. The same Latino, black, and other groups that are struggling to gain some measure of control over the educational process in their own community are also the ones whose rights are most often denied or abridged within the school itself. For example, recent analyses have demonstrated that, both in the North and the South, a disproportionate number of black and Latino students are suspended or expelled from school. This cannot be explained by the number of, say, "minority" students within the schools; nor can it be explained by the acts the students "committed." In fact, even when the same acts were committed by white, black, Latino, and other groups, the minority students were those more usually suspended or expelled.[5] Therefore, we need to be quite cautious about expecting too much from legal maneuvers by themselves. Yet, as I shall point out here, this does not mean we should ignore legal avenues of redress. In fact, there are not a few legal precedents that may be helpful in making schools more responsive to culturally distinct students.

## The Limitations of Legal Action

Mann and Molnar are correct when they describe the practical limitations that legal action has in getting at the root causes of the abridgment of democratic rights in schools. While they agree that litigation is a useful tactic in that it acts to "restrain some school administrators and helps achieve or consolidate certain important rights," they go on to argue that:

(a) The Supreme Court and lower courts cannot be relied upon to interpret the

[5]Michael Roth and Henry Lufler, Jr. "An Overview of School Suspensions and Expulsions in Wisconsin." Madison, Wisconsin: Center for Public Representation, May 1976. (Mimeographed.)

Constitution progressively. (b) Litigation is expensive, frequently too expensive for students and their families. (c) In their rulings the courts often assert that the particulars of each case warrant different conclusions. This effectively blocks the general acceptance of many rulings and necessitates more litigation. A single successful court case leads to only the smallest and most specific remedy possible. (d) Most students, parents, and school officials are ignorant of the legal rights of students. Illegal violations of students' rights are routinely accepted in many schools because of ignorance and because such rights fly head-on into the prevailing culture of the schools and the culture of the society which sustains the schools. . . . (e) Finally, there is no reason to believe that any court action would or could lead to the establishment of the kinds of rights and responsibilities we have proposed for students [i.e., studying and engaging in progressive social action against oppression and imperialism as part of their education].[6]

However, the important thing to note here is that educators who are concerned with the abridgment of rights in schools must realize the intricate connections between the lack of democratic rights within the formal institutions of schooling and the struggle for such rights by all dominated people in this society. This is not to say that legal action to prevent abuses of constitutional liberties in schools should stop. Rather, I want to argue that without connecting the advances in dealing with the quality of educational life in this one arena with the long and difficult educational, economic, and political struggle in the larger arena, we are apt to be satisfied with rather small, often insignificant, and perhaps ultimately ephemeral "progress."

What is critical at this time, though, is the establishment of mechanisms through which these repeated failures to uphold rights can be challenged. Ways need to be found to create an interface between the student and the bureaucratic structure of the institution. That is, people such as student advocates — parents, lawyers, etc. — need to be given legitimacy within the school so that they can assist students in challenging such things as unwarranted labeling and tracking, procedural concerns involving suspension and expulsion, freedom of access to politically and racially progressive curricula and literature, and so forth.

In doing this, we need to transfer the burden of proof from the pupil to the school in any regulations regarding substantive rights. That is, school officials should be required to demonstrate the reasonableness of their denials of rights and, as well, should be able to show a strong relationship between personal and group freedom and so called "disruption."[7] Let me reiterate, however, that the establishment of such legal mechanisms should *not* be viewed

6John S. Mann and Alex Molnar for the Radical Caucus. "On Student Rights." *Educational Leadership* 31 (8): 670; May 1974.

7Bonnie Cook Freeman. "Trends, Conflicts, and Implications in Student Rights." Vernon F. Haubrich and Michael W. Apple, editors. *Schooling and the Rights of Children*. Berkeley: Mc-Cutchan and The National Society for the Study of Education, 1975.

as an end in itself. These are tactical decisions for making progress in a relatively limited area of schooling. The legal advocacy needs to be linked with other forms of activity, both educational and political, so that these advances are connected to the larger movement for racial, sexual, and economic justice in other institutions.

There are decided benefits from such a strategy. The legal mechanisms provide one set of means for parents, students, members of oppressed groups, child advocates, and others to insert themselves on a local level in confronting some of the established practices of our educational institutions. Now the very fact that the issues are dealt with piecemeal, student case by student case, may make it difficult for people to see a larger pattern of oppression beyond the individual situation; but, because the issues *are* so close, the concrete need for doing something, for inserting oneself, is enhanced.

While educators should lead the courts and the legal system on such questions as student rights, there are precedents already extant that may provide possibilities for such action now while more basic challenges are articulated and people are building a supportive base for other forms of emancipating activity. Therefore, I want to examine certain legal precedents that may make it easier for all of us to find avenues to begin to raise challenges.

## Some Possible Precedents in Student Rights

The question of due process has become one of the more involved issues surrounding schooling and children's rights and is the one which most students seem to focus upon. Its basis lies in the Fourteenth Amendment which provides that no state shall deprive an individual of his or her life, liberty, or property without due process. Legally, it is possible to delineate two types of due process: procedural and substantive. As the name suggests, procedural due process deals with the process by which an individual is judged. In principle, it requires three broad and basic factors: (a) the individual must be given proper notice that he or she is about to be deprived of personal life, liberty, or property; (b) it is necessary that he or she be given an opportunity to be heard; and (c) the hearing itself must be conducted fairly.[8]

Substantive due process is less concerned with the formal means of justice; rather it is concerned with specific ends and the means used to achieve them. That is, the state's objective itself must be valid and the means it uses must be "reasonably calculated to achieve the objective." Mandatory vaccinations to ensure good health usually provide an example of such means and goals.[9] Questions of students' rights pertain to both types of due process, though

[8] Kern Alexander *et al. Public School Law: Cases and Materials.* St. Paul, Minnesota: West Publishing Co., 1969. p. 539.

[9] *Ibid.,* p. 540.

procedural issues seem to have dominated recently. As I shall soon note, however, controversies over substantive due process could, in fact, raise quite important questions about the process of educating "minority" students itself and may make a strong impact on the very character of schools themselves in the near future. To make this clear, let us first examine selected but important precedents that have established elements of due process for students in schools.

Recent decisions in the Supreme Court and elsewhere have slowly but surely established a judicial climate for constitutional challenges to the regulation of student conduct by school authorities.[10] The 1967 *In re Gault* decision is a case in point where a broad impact has already been felt upon a school's decisions regarding student conduct. Swift summarizes the case and its implications well:

> The case recognized a juvenile's constitutional right to certain procedural safeguards such as the right to cross-examination in a criminal action against him in juvenile court. The court felt that juvenile proceedings designed to provide a guidance function were failing in that duty and in fact were resulting in summarily imposed criminal punishment. The same argument [can be] applied to disciplinary actions against students resulting in their suspension, transfer, or expulsion from schools.[11]

The *Tinker* decision provides yet another exceptionally important instance. The case dealt with the suspension of students by school authorities for wearing black armbands to protest the Vietnam War. The Supreme Court's ruling on this is rather instructive. The court argued that the school administration in Des Moines had wrongfully restricted the students' constitutional rights because it had not shown that the student protest would significantly disrupt the educational atmosphere of the school. That is:

> In order for the state in the person of school officials to justify prohibition of a particular expression of opinion, it must be able to show that its action was caused by something more than a mere desire to avoid the discomfort and unpleasantness that always accompany an unpopular viewpoint. Certainly where there is no finding and no showing that the exercise of the forbidden right would materially and substantially interfere with the requirements of appropriate discipline in the operation of a school, the appropriation cannot be sustained.[12]

We should note here that *Tinker* is partially problematic in that it does not

---

[10]Larry E. Swift. "The Role of the High School Principal as Affected by Some Recent Developments in the Law of Student Rights." Larry E. Swift, editor. *Student Rights and Responsibilities.* Bellingham, Washington: Northwest District Administrators Association, 1972. p. 46.

[11]*Ibid.,* p. 47.

[12]Tinker *v* Des Moines Independent Community School District, 393 U.S. 503 at 509 (1969), as quoted in: *Ibid.,* p. 48.

define clearly *what* activity is to be construed as disruptive, nor does it give clear guidelines as to *who* is the final arbiter in deciding whether student activity is substantially disruptive. In point of fact, as Mann and Molnar point out, some activities may have to be "disruptive" (as institutionally defined) if they are to have a significant impact on the taken-for-granted regularities of the school. This does point to the argument raised earlier in this paper, though, about how important it is for the burden of proof concerning disruption or other rights issues to be laid upon school authorities not on the students or their advocates.

The *reasoning* employed in the *Tinker* opinion is critical, however, and rests upon the thesis that the rights guaranteed by the First Amendment are actually "essential to an effective educational process in a democracy rather than a disruption of that process."[13] In essence, controversy, diversity, and open argumentation are to be looked upon not as problems to be eliminated at whatever cost, but as signs of a responsible educative environment. While there have been recent cases that have narrowed the *Tinker* and *Gault* rulings, one thing is clear, the courts are in this area to stay and will be used again and again to test heretofore unquestioned school authority.

But even with these possible procedural and substantive precedents, as I demonstrated earlier in this discussion, schools may still not actually tell students and parents what their rights are. Nor may many schools act to uphold these guarantees. In fact, given both the relatively slow pace of serious acceptance of student (and teacher) rights in many schools and the conservative nature of the curriculum materials found in school districts throughout the country, students themselves have often attempted to bring into school and distribute materials that are more representative of their own culture's point of view. This will probably be necessary in the future as well. That is, the students themselves can and do act as catalysts in altering school experience by bringing into the institution and distributing material and resources that honestly represent the culture and history of particular classes and groups of people. In some areas of the country this distribution may be against the expressed or implied wishes of the school itself and may generate a considerable amount of conflict. Because of this, it is essential that we have some sense of the rights students have to distribute "non-school" material.

Phay and Rogister, in their interesting analysis of student rights to distribute such "non-school" literature, describe the types of restriction schools may impose on such distribution:

The First and Fourteenth Amendments to the United States Constitution (and

---

[13]Richard L. Berkman. "Students in Court: Free Speech and the Function of Schooling in America." *Education and the Legal Structure.* Reprint series number 6, *Harvard Educational Review,* 1971. p. 49.

similar provisions in state constitutions) guarantee a right of free speech and expression that extends to students in schools. This right is not absolute but limited. The difficulty is in establishing precisely what is protected speech and beyond school control. The courts have decided enough cases within the last five years to permit defining with some clarity those instances when school limitations on the distribution of literature are constitutionally permissible and when they are not. The permissible limitations can be divided into four broad categories: (1) the school can limit the distribution of literature if the distribution will result or can reasonably be forecast to result in "material and substantial disruption of school activities"; (2) the school can set limits on the time, place, and manner of the distribution; (3) the school can prohibit the distribution of materials that are obscene, libelous, or inflammatory; and (4) the school can prohibit distribution when the distribution involves the violation of school rules, although the literature itself may be protected from school rules prohibiting distribution.[14]

While the courts have ruled that the distribution of "provocative" material by students can be limited by school authorities, this does *not* give school personnel blanket authority to eliminate honest material. In fact, quite the opposite is the case. Here is one area where the burden of proof *is* on the school, not on the individual or group of students. School authorities must show specifically that "material and substantial disruption resulted or was likely to result from students' exercise of their First Amendment freedoms in a particular situation."[15] Thus a school's psychological discomfort over competing conceptions of social or cultural life is not enough for a school to abridge a student's constitutional freedoms; nor, as the *Tinker* case put it, is an "undifferentiated fear or apprehension of disturbance enough to overcome the right to freedom of expression." The court went on, arguing that schools must not construe a student's freedom of expression too narrowly. The court's basic point is critically important to my argument about the culture schools distribute through the "official" curriculum. In essence, "School officials do not possess absolute authority over their students. . . . In our system, students may not be regarded as closed-circuit recipients of only that which the state chooses to communicate."[16]

Now this is an important political question, one which I have examined at greater length elsewhere, for it raises the issue of whose knowledge it is that schools distribute.[17] In short, what social and economic groups actually benefit from the school curriculum? While this is quite a complex problem, let it

---

[14]Robert E. Phay and George T. Rogister, Jr. "Student Distribution of Non-School Literature." *NOPLE School Law Journal* 4 (2): 125; 1974.

[15]*Ibid.*, p. 133.

[16]Quoted in: *Ibid.*, p. 126.

[17]Michael W. Apple and Nancy R. King. "What Do Schools Teach?" James B. Macdonald and William Gephart, editors. *Humanism and Education.* Berkeley: McCutchan Publishing Corp., 1977.

suffice to say that the British critical sociologist of education, Michael F.D. Young, is quite insightful when he argues that "those in positions of power will attempt to define what is taken as knowledge, how accessible to different groups any knowledge is, and what are the accepted relationships between different knowledge areas and between those who have access to them and make them available."[18] In other words, some social groups' knowledge becomes school knowledge, and in the process is given legitimacy as "real" or "important" knowledge, while other groups' knowledge is considered commonsensical or "unimportant" and, hence, is in essence denied social legitimacy. And whether a specific group's knowledge is represented in school is strongly related to that particular social community's power in the larger social arena. Thus, given students' continuing attempts to bring honest material into our educational institutions, it is important to strengthen the rights of students from less powerful groups if we are, in fact, to alter whose knowledge ultimately gets into schools.

But it is not merely the protection of students' rights to bring in different and often provocative cultural and historical material that should concern us. As I mentioned, minority students are often those who are more apt to be given "punishments" like expulsion for bringing in honest material or for other actions. Because of this it would be helpful to be aware of certain of their procedural rights in schools. While these will differ from place to place and from grade level to grade level, there are certain precedents established in college and university settings, some of which have filtered down to and made a significant impact upon high schools, that generally describe the types of rights culturally different students and others often have. It would not be at all odd to expect them to take hold slowly in elementary schools as well. These rights often include:

1. Notice of charges against a student prior to the imposition of discipline, such as expulsion

2. Notice of the charges must be timely, that is, without unreasonable delay (waiting in limbo can be a form of punishment, obviously) and with sufficient time to prepare a defense

3. An opportunity for a hearing

4. An impartial hearing committee or arbiter

5. The decision of the committee or individual must be based upon "substantial evidence"

6. The right to hear all of the evidence against an individual *before* he or she makes a defense

[18]Michael F.D. Young. "An Approach to the Study of Curricula as Socially Organized Knowledge." Michael F.D. Young, editor. *Knowledge and Control*. London: Collier-Macmillan, 1971. p. 32.

7. The right to testify and present evidence and witnesses

8. The right to know and rebut the evidence and the witnesses against you

9. The making of a transcript of the proceedings

10. Freedom from unreasonable coercion; this may include even the physical setting of the room if it is designed to make a student uncomfortable, and it is especially important with relatively young students

11. Written notice of the decision

12. Right to appeal.[19]

It is quite possible that the courts will extend the coverage of such due process as those just noted to any case where some representative of a public institution significantly influences another individual's life or future fortunes.

It is here that procedural and substantive due process begin to merge. This merger may have a profound impact in school decision making. The question raised in the background more and more is not "merely" one of procedural due process, where the student is accorded the rights usually held by adults in general or by those adults placed under arrest or being charged with a crime. Rather, the climate created by cases like *Gault*, and by many of the decisions to which I have not pointed concerning a "patient's" right to be given the appropriate psychological or psychiatric treatment if he or she is to be confined, are beginning to establish a framework that will necessitate substantive justice to be done as well as procedural justice.[20] That is, anything that is done to the juvenile "offender" must be shown to actually help.

The implications for education are strikingly important. Let us take one example, the *Lessard* case to illuminate the possible ramifications. The *Wisconsin v. Lessard* case was concerned with the question of commitment to a mental hospital. A three judge federal appellate court in Milwaukee extended the protections secured in the *Gault, Kent,* and similar cases when it ruled on the *Lessard* example. According to one juvenile judge, in the background of the court's arguments was a position that, on constitutional grounds: (a) the state must show a compelling reason for interfering with the rights of a person; (b) a "least interference principle" shall hold — that is, that of all the treatments available for a person, the one that *least* abridges an individual's rights is to be employed, and, most importantly; (c) the state

---

[19]Michael Nussbaum. *Student Legal Rights: What They Are and How To Protect Them.* New York: Harper & Row, Publishers, 1970. pp. 46-55. Copyright © 1970 by Michael Nussbaum. Reprinted by permission of Harper & Row, Publishers. For one state's model code for dealing with these rights in schools, see: Larry E. Swift, "The Role of the High School Principal as Affected by Some Recent Developments in the Law of Student Rights," *op. cit.*

[20]Justine Wise Polier. "Juvenile Justice Confounded." *Inequality in Education* 13: 65; December 1972.

must show reasonable evidence that the treatment will be effective.[21] The Supreme Court ultimately ruled against *Lessard* on technical grounds. However, there will be other cases that will provide potent challenges.

Now while keeping in mind that the *Lessard* example deals with the confinement of a person to a mental hospital, let us place this legal reasoning in an educational framework and apply it to a common educational practice. Perhaps the best example is that of tracking or variants of it and the social and economic class and culturally biased labeling that results from it. Here a school district would be called upon to present evidence at a hearing, showing that the specific placement of a child will in fact be helpful and will not abridge his or her other rights more than an alternative program which is more responsive to his or her culture and desires. Given the extant evidence on tracking or even placing students in so-called "slow groups," educators may be hard pressed to support their decisions. The reasoning employed here is not as outlandish as it seems.

For example, precedent for the establishment of the right to a hearing before one is to be tracked or perhaps even ability grouped may be found in the litigation surrounding the recent Pennsylvania case making it the state's duty to provide public education for retarded children. Here the court ordered that before a "retarded" student's educational assignment can be changed the parents must be given notice and the opportunity to be heard. Furthermore, this same notice and possibility of a hearing is to be extended every two years, or every year if the parents so request. The ruling also extends to the parent and the child the right to independent evaluation of the child's capabilities and full access to all records of the child kept by the school. Other procedural guarantees include the rights to representation (a lawyer, child advocate, etc.), calling and examining any person employed by the school district, and the presentation of witnesses and counter evidence. Finally, and perhaps most significantly for substantive justice, not only must the decision of the hearing be supported by written findings of facts, but *the sole criterion for the decision is to be whether the education program in question is the appropriate program for that particular child.*[22]

This accomplishes some rather important things. It provides a formal way for parents to hold schools "accountable" for the specific educative settings

[21]For further discussion of these points see the excellent treatment in: Nicholas N. Kittrie. *The Right to Be Different: Deviance and Enforced Therapy.* Baltimore: Johns Hopkins, 1971.

[22]Thomas K. Gilhool. "The Uses of Litigation: The Right of Retarded Children to a Free Public Education." *Peabody Journal of Education* 50: 125; January 1973.

[23]*Ibid.,* p. 127. The fact that this could lead to pressure for some of the more vulgar forms of accountability is worth remembering. There may very well be latent problems, hence, with these gains in rights. See, e.g.: Michael W. Apple. "The Adequacy of Systems Management Procedures in Education." Ralph Smith, editor. *Regaining Educational Leadership.* New York: John Wiley, 1975. pp. 104-21.

and programs for children.[23] It also gives a more formal standing to the child advocate or, as he or she might be called, an educational ombudsperson who acts to protect the constitutional rights of children in schools. Such a position is being created informally but rather rapidly, especially in urban areas, where lawyers, for instance, are placing themselves as an interface between the student and the bureaucracy, thereby providing a mechanism for countering some of the very real class, racial, and sexual biases that are so prevalent in many schools.

Following the precedent in Pennsylvania, it is quite possible that courts will begin to expand their area of concern into decisions involving specific academic programs. That is, the courts may command school systems to establish specific curricular programs for socially and ethnically different children with a high probability of success. This may be further extended in cases involving individuals. In some states, for instance, the climate is ripe for a judicial decision that would argue that it is a school district's responsibility to design educational experiences *specifically* created for an individual child.[24] In other words, the court could rule that the state or its representatives have a legal obligation to establish a quality and responsive educative environment for each child under its purview. This might mean, thus, that especially for what schools like to label "difficult" or "different" children, there must be established an individual program in or out of the formal school setting that the student would find satisfying and stimulating, and that would have a high probability of success. For those of us specifically interested in politically and culturally progressive out of school educational experiences, this could provide a good deal of help.

It should be noted that the federal courts have indicated in several decisions that they will not as yet consider questions of the quality of education outside of, say, the issue of segregation; nevertheless, as I argued earlier, there has been a significant change in the climate of opinion in many lower judicial cases in some areas of the country.[25] This change is heightened by the fact that schools are increasingly being compared to other state controlled "total institutions" such as mental hospitals, thereby providing a potent analogy for use in arguing from court precedents in mental commitment cases and the like.[26] Precedents based on premises such as these may prove

[24]Lecture given by Juvenile Court Judge Ervin Bruner at a seminar on: "Schooling and the Rights of Children." Madison: University of Wisconsin, January 31, 1973.

[25]Thomas K. Gilhool, "The Uses of Litigation," *op. cit.,* p. 125. See also the discussion of the Supreme Court's recent movement away from substantive due process rulings in Wallace Mendelson. "From Warren to Burger: The Rise and Decline of Substantive Equal Protection." *The American Political Science Review* 66: 1226-33; December 1972. For a rather thorough examination of substantive and procedural rulings in student rights as they differ throughout the country, see: Bruce Szudy. "Student Rights and Constitutional Law." M.S. thesis. Madison: University of Wisconsin, 1974.

[26]Cf.: Philip Jackson. *Life in Classrooms.* New York: Holt, Rinehart & Winston, 1968; and Erving Goffman. *Asylums.* New York: Doubleday & Company, Inc., 1961.

increasingly important in the current and future argumentation over making educational environments more responsive and just to students of those groups that have historically had their rights abridged the most.

## Conclusion

While these precedents are not uniform throughout the country and are not always followed even where they should be, it would be wise for us to face their implications now. Schools have been rather lax in their concern for constitutionally guaranteed rights, perhaps because of their belief that they are providing guidance rather than punishment, or that they are always attempting to help not hinder a young person's difficult problem of finding oneself in a complex institutional setting. However, such a position is less than tenable today. In fact, as I have noted before, the ways educators have of "helping" children, of ameliorating the "problems children have," may not ultimately help as much as supposed. Rather, they may rest on ideologically biased presuppositions which, when put into practice within school settings (in terms of differentiated curricula, labeling, and the like), have a decidedly harmful effect on the children upon whom these helping models focus.[27] Mercer's masterful examination of the labeling process involved in mental testing, for example, offers a case in point where expertise resting upon conservative social and educational ideologies *created* deviance in schools rather than actually solving the problems themselves. The impact of this process on minority students was devastating. We have much to learn from this about the importance of legal mechanisms to protect students from some very real harm.[28]

The growth of the child advocacy position throughout the country and the concomitant rise in an adversary relationship between schools and youth are but a few signs (ones that I perceive to be healthy and necessary) that schools cannot be immune to procedural or substantive justice in their educational functions. Perhaps we can learn something from the reasoning in the Tinker decision quoted earlier in this discussion. Not only may conflict, dissension, and argumentation be important to the educational process itself, but they also may act as one means to force institutions like schools to be more responsive to their most important constituency, students.

Yet we also have a good deal to learn from the reasoning used in *Tinker* in another context. Conflict and dissent are important for justice in society as well and we must insert ourselves into the larger struggle to deal with this.

[27]Cf.: Michael W. Apple, "Commonsense Categories and Curriculum Thought," *op. cit.*

[28]Jane R. Mercer. *Labeling the Mentally Retarded*. Berkeley: The University of California Press, 1973. See also: Jane R. Mercer. "A Policy Statement on Assessment Procedures and the Rights of Children." *Harvard Educational Review* 44: 125-41; February 1974.

The concern of committed curriculists and other educators for justice and the quality of life within the institution of schooling must be mirrored by a similar concern for justice and the quality of life distributed by and in the other dominant institutions in our society. Thus, legal mechanisms may be a beginning; they cannot be the end.

# 4

# Anthropological Foundations of Education That Is Multicultural

Carl A. Grant

*If one were to offer men to choose out of all the customs in the world such as seemed to them the best, they would examine the whole number, and end by preferring their own; so convinced are they that their own usages surpass those of all others.*

— *Herodotus*, **The Persian Wars**, Book III, Chapter 38

For too long, American education has demonstrated the truth of Herodotus' observation of almost 2500 years ago. Until recently, our schools have sought to "Americanize" students, denying the diversity of cultures and languages which students brought with them — asking them, instead, to check their diversity at the schoolhouse door, and in many instances trying to convince them not to reclaim it when they left.

Recent realignment of political power in the United States has, however, forced us to recognize that we are not a homogeneous nation. Calls for Black Rights, Puerto Rican Rights, Women's Rights, Grey Power, Red Power, and so on, have forced us to recognize that we are indeed a culturally pluralistic nation. And with this recognition, we have been forced to reexamine our educational system. Out of this reexamination has evolved the concept of multicultural education.

Education that is multicultural[1] is a concept predicated upon a fundamental belief that all people must be accorded respect, regardless of their
social, ethnic, cultural, and religious background. It is manifested in an educational process that neither advocates nor tolerates the heating up of the old
"melting pot" nor the creation of multi "monocultural" educational programs. Instead, education that is multicultural includes such features as the
following: (a) staffing composition and patterns throughout the organizational hierarchy that reflect the pluralistic nature of American society; (b) curricula that are appropriate, flexible, unbiased, and that incorporate the contributions of all cultural groups; (c) affirmation of the languages of various
cultural groups as different rather than deficient; (d) instructional materials
that are free of bias, omissions, and stereotypes; that are inclusive rather
than supplementary; and that portray individuals from different cultural
groups in a variety of different occupational and social roles.

I believe that what we have learned in disciplines such as anthropology,
sociology, and psychology support the basic tenets of education that is multicultural. Although these disciplines often have overlapping areas of interest,
they do not always ask the same questions. Therefore, in this paper, I propose
to focus solely upon the relationship between anthropology and education
that is multicultural.

Almost 50 years ago, anthropologist Franz Boas made the following com-
ments about his field:

> Anthropology is often considered a collection of curious facts, telling about the
> peculiar appearance of exotic people and describing their strange customs and be-
> liefs. It is looked at as an entertaining diversion, apparently without any bearing
> upon the conduct of life of civilized communities.
>
> This opinion is mistaken. More than that, I hope to demonstrate that a *clear un-
> derstanding of the principles of anthropology illuminates the social processes of our
> own times and may show us, if we are ready to listen to its teachings, what to do and
> what to avoid.*[2]

Anthropology and education share a common area of concern: the transmission of culture. With the recognition, and to a lesser degree acceptance, of
the United States as a culturally pluralistic nation,[3] it behooves us to reexamine the relationship between anthropology and education (" . . . *a clear
understanding of the principles of anthropology illuminates the social pro-*

---

[1]For a discussion of why this term is preferred to "multicultural education" see: Carl A.
Grant. "Education That Is Multicultural — Isn't That What We Mean?" Submitted manuscript.

[2]Franz Boas. *Anthropology and Modern Life*. New York: W.W. Norton & Company, 1928.
p. 11. (Emphasis added.)

[3]See, for instance: "No One Model American." *Journal of Teacher Education* 24: 264;
Winter 1973.

*cesses of our own times . . .* "). In addition, I should like to propose that what we have learned from anthropology has important implications for education that is multicultural (" . . . *may show us, if we are ready to listen to its teachings, what to do and what to avoid* ").

## Culture and Education

Writing of anthropology's recent accomplishments, A.L. Kroeber said:

The most significant accomplishment of anthropology in the first half of the 20th Century has been the extension and clarification of the concept of culture. The idea that culture — a society's customs, traditions, tools, and ways of thinking — plays the dominant part in shaping the development of human beings, and therefore ought to be the central concern of anthropology, did not originate in our century; its importance had been recognized by the great English anthropologist Edward B. Taylor in 1871. But during the past 50 years the concept has been given a wide and consistent application which has immensely advanced the growth of anthropological science.[4]

The definitions of culture are many, but are essentially similar to that used by Kroeber. Clyde Kluckhohn and William Kelly, for instance, have defined culture as all the " . . . historically created designs for living, explicit and implicit, rational, irrational, and nonrational, which exist at any given time as potential guides for the behavior of men."[5] Melville Herskovits has stated that, "Defined as the man-made part of the environment, culture is essentially a construct that describes the total body of belief, behavior, knowledge, sanctions, values, and goals that mark the way of life of any people."[6]

Herskovits further notes that, "The aspects of the learning experience which mark off man from other creatures, and by means of which, initially, and in later life, he achieves competence in his culture, may be called *enculturation.*"[7] And from this follows his definition of education as, ". . . that part of the enculturative experience that, through the learning process, equips an individual to take his place as an adult member of his society."[8]

It is this process of enculturation that provides the areas of common concern between anthropology and education. Or as George Spindler has written:

[4]A.L. Kroeber. "Anthropology." *Scientific American* 183:87; September 1950.

[5]Clyde Kluckhohn and William H. Kelly. "The Concept of Culture." Ralph Linton, editor. *The Science of Man in the World Crisis.* New York: Columbia University Press, 1945. p. 97.

[6]Melville J. Herskovits. *Man and His Works: The Science of Cultural Anthropology.* New York: Alfred A. Knopf, Inc., 1966. p. 625. Copyright © 1947 by Melville J. Herskovits. Reprinted by permission of Alfred A. Knopf, Inc.

[7]*Ibid.,* p. 39.

[8]*Ibid.,* p. 310.

The anthropology of education is an attempt to understand better what the teacher is doing and of what the educational process consists, by studying the teacher as a cultural transmitter and education as a process of cultural transmission. Some interesting results appear from such analyses. For instance, it becomes clear that even the most fair-minded teachers are highly selective of the values they communicate to students and are equally selective with respect to what values they screen out from what students might potentially communicate to them. It also seems clear on the basis of such approaches that teachers, in fact whole educational programs, frequently communicate assumptions and outlooks about human relations that are not in agreement with their declared goals.[9]

I have elsewhere discussed in depth the role of the teacher as a transmitter or mediator of culture.[10] Therefore, I should like to treat, not merely the anthropology of education, but the implications of anthropological theory and research for education that is multicultural.

I propose that anthropological theory and research provide firm support for education that is multicultural. This support comes from three areas of anthropological knowledge: (a) knowledge of the universals in human experience, that is, what all people have in common; (b) recognition and respect for cultural diversity; and (c) studies of how individuals (particularly children) are socialized into their society. I shall focus here on the first two of these three areas of knowledge because (a) it is necessary to understand fully these two areas of knowledge before one can begin to investigate the many facets of socialization in a pluralistic society, and (b) through an examination of both the universals and the diversity of human experience and culture we can establish a firm basis for the respect for all peoples that is the cornerstone of education that is multicultural.

## Universals in Human Experience

Most anthropological research has been devoted to the study of differences: how humans differ from animals and how humans differ from each other. Humans have long been interested in observing and reporting upon groups of people whose modes of living varied from their own; Caesar's writings on Gaul and Tacitus' on the Germans are but two examples of this interest. Likewise, Linnaeus began the construction of a formal system for categorizing living things, and the writings of Darwin raised the problem of where in the animal kingdom to place Homo sapiens. Our concern here, however, is not with differences, but with similarities. First, we shall examine

---

[9]George D. Spindler. "Current Anthropology." George D. Spindler, editor. *Education and Culture.* New York: Holt, Rinehart and Winston, Inc., 1963. p. 41.

[10]Carl A. Grant. "Mediator of Culture." Paper in progress.

what it is that differentiates humans from other animals. Then, we shall see what it is that all humans have in common.

That humans and other animals have much in common cannot be denied. Human and animal societies share much in common, both in form and function. Both make internal differentiations on the basis of some trait such as age or size and have a cooperative aspect. Similarly, such functions as care of the young and protection against predators characterize both groups.[11] There are, however, two things which differentiate between humans and other animals: humans possess both language and culture.

Language is a system of arbitrary vocal symbols which are used by members of a social group to facilitate group cooperation and interaction. It is also the means by which a given way of life achieves both change and continuity via the effectuation of the learning process.[12] And Leslie A. White notes that, "All human behavior originates in the use of symbols. It was the symbol which transformed our anthropoid ancestors into men and made them human."[13] Apes, because they have no language are unable to continue their experiences in word and thought.

Language then is one of the characteristics that distinguishes humans from other animals; and language provides the basis for the existence of that other distinguishing characteristic: culture. In his discussion of symbols as the basis of language, White says:

All culture (civilization) depends upon the symbol. It was the exercise of the symbolic faculty that brought culture into existence and it is the use of symbols that makes the perpetuation of culture possible. Without the symbol there would be no culture, and man would be merely an animal, not a human being.[14]

Harry Hoijer affirms this when he says, " . . . a society lacking language would have no means of assuring the continuity of behavior and learning necessary to the creation of culture. Human society, without culture, would be reduced to the level of present-day ape societies."[15]

Having granted that it is language and culture which distinguish humans from other animals, we may still not easily concede that language and culture are the universals of human experience. Do we not find people speaking many different tongues and living in many different manners? Are there not

---

[11]Herskovits, *Man and His Works*, *op. cit.*, p. 37.

[12]Edgar H. Sturtevant. *An Introduction to Linguistic Science*. New Haven: Yale University Press, 1947. p.2.

[13]Leslie A. White. *The Science of Culture*. New York: Farrar Straus & Giroux, Inc., 1949. Copyright © 1949 by Leslie A. White. Copyright renewed © 1976 by Crocker National Bank as Executor of the Estate of Leslie A. White.

[14]*Ibid.*, p. 73.

[15]Harry Hoijer. "Language and Writing." Harry L. Shapiro, editor. *Man, Culture, and Society*. New York: Oxford University Press, 1971. p. 269.

a myriad of both languages and cultures? Certainly all people do not share a common language. However, all languages have a great deal in common: (a) All languages have a well-defined system of speech sounds which are finite in number and clearly distinguishable from each other, and which are put together in accordance with definite rules to form words, phrases, and sentences. (b) All human societies have a vocabulary which is sufficiently detailed and comprehensive to meet every need which is likely to arise; and in the event that new items are invented or borrowed, these vocabularies all appear to be indefinitely expandable. (c) All languages have a definite system of grammar. Thus, although all people do not share a common language, language in its broadest sense is common to all people.

Likewise, although there exists a myriad of diverse cultures, all cultures are constructed according to what Clark Wissler has termed "the universal culture pattern."[16] As Ralph Linton has noted, "Behind the seemingly endless diversity of culture patterns there is a fundamental uniformity."[17] The foregoing is not meant to suggest, however, that all cultures are the same. Rather, as George Peter Murdock notes, "What cultures are found to have in common is a uniform system of classification, not a fund of identical elements."[18] He further notes that, ". . . even today it is not generally recognized how numerous and diverse are the elements common to all known cultures."[19] Among those common elements which he notes are age-grading, calendar, eschatology, funeral rites, and kinship nomenclature.

That all cultures have common elements suggests that while all people do not share a common culture, all people have something in common. Kluckhohn concurs in this belief when he notes that, ". . . the mere existence of universals after so many millennia of culture history and in such diverse environments suggests that they correspond to something extremely deep in man's nature and/or are necessary conditions to social life."[20]

Murdock suggests that the existence of a universal culture pattern may rest in part in a belief in the "psychic unity of mankind." He describes this as:

. . . the assumption that all peoples now living or of whom we possess substantial historical records, irrespective of differences in geography and physique, are essentially alike in their basic psychological equipment and mechanism, and that cultural

---

[16]Cited by George Peter Murdock in: "The Common Denominator of Cultures." Ralph Linton, editor. *The Science of Man in the World Crisis*. New York: Columbia University Press, 1945. p. 125.

[17]Ralph Linton. "Universal Ethical Principles: An Anthropological View." Ruth N. Anshen, editor. *Moral Principles of Action*. New York: Harper & Row, Publishers, 1952. p. 646.

[18]Murdock, "The Common Denominator of Cultures," *op. cit.*, p. 125.

[19]*Ibid.*, p. 124.

[20]Clyde Kluckhohn. "Education, Values, and Anthropological Relativity." Richard Kluckhohn, editor. *Culture and Behavior*. New York: Free Press, 1962. p. 296.

differences between them reflect only the different responses of essentially similar organisms to unlike stimuli or conditions.[21]

Each culture is thus merely a somewhat distinct answer to the same questions which are posed by such things as human biology. The basic similarities in all human biology are much more massive in number than the variation. Each human society must provide ways for dealing with such universal circumstances as the elementary biological needs for food and warmth, the existence of two sexes, and the helplessness of infants. In addition to the ways in which human societies respond to those problems posed by nature, all cultures share some broad resemblances in value content. The incest taboo, for instance, is essentially universal. Likewise, while suffering (punishment or discipline) may be a means to societal or individual ends, no culture places a value on suffering as an end in itself. Thus, no culture is wholly isolated or disparate, since "most of the patterns of all cultures crystallize around the same foci."[22] Rather, each culture is comparable and related to all other cultures.

Thus, although there exists a great diversity in language and culture, all of humankind also shares a great deal in common. Anthropology's contribution to this recognition is aptly summarized by Kluckhohn:

At the same time one must never forget that cultural differences, real and important though they are, are still so many variations on themes supplied by raw human nature. The common understandings between men of different cultures are very broad, very general, and very easily obscured by language and many other observable symbols. True universals or near-universals are apparently few in number. But they seem to be as deep-going as they are rare. Anthropology's facts attest that the phrase "A common humanity" is in no sense meaningless.[23]

## Cultural Diversity

Despite the fact that anthropologists have pointed out cultural universals and written about the factual basis for a belief in "a common humanity," most people tend to view other cultures via ethnocentrism. As defined by Herskovits, "Ethonocentrism is the point of view that one's own way of life is to be preferred to all others."[24] Ethnocentrism is the mechanism that frequently leads people to the conclusion that one culture is somehow "better" than another.

One of the manners in which this ethnocentric ranking of cultures mani-

---

[21]Murdock, "The Common Denominator of Cultures," *op. cit.*, p. 126.

[22]Kluckhohn, "Education, Values, and Anthropological Relativity," *op. cit.*, p. 294.

[23]*Ibid.*, p. 297.

[24]Herskovits, *Man and His Works, op. cit.*, p. 68.

fests itself is in the use of the word "primitive" to describe certain cultures. As Herskovits explains, "The word 'primitive' came into use when anthropological theory was dominated by an evolutionary approach that equated living peoples, outside the stream of European culture, with the early inhabitants of the earth."[25] The use of "primitive" is not only widespread among the general populace, but is pervasive in anthropology, as evidenced by such titles as *Primitive Religion, Sex and Temperament in Three Primitive Societies,* and *Primitive Art.*[26] Or as Herskovits notes:

The conception implicit in such pervades our thinking more than we realize. It colors many of the judgments we draw about the way of life of native peoples with whom the expansion of European and American controls have brought us into contact. When we speak or write of the living customs of the American Indian or African or South Seas peoples in the past tense, we imply that their customs are in some way earlier than our own. We are treating their cultures as though they were unchanging when, as we have seen, one of the basic generalizations about culture is that no body of custom is static. No matter how conservative a people may be, we find on investigation that their way of life is not the same as it was in earlier times.[27]

Herskovits concludes that in the etymological sense of the word, the use of "primitive" to describe present day cultures is a misnomer, and that "there is no justification for regarding any living group as our contemporary ancestors."[28]

The use of the word primitive has, unfortunately, not been limited to use as a descriptor of time sequence. It has also been fraught with value judgment and used in conjuction with such terms as "savage," "uncivilized," and "barbaric" to demean/ridicule cultures which are different from that of the person who chooses to throw such an epithet. Yet, ironically, it is anthropology, for all its initial emphasis on cultural differences, which has, in the 20th century, in part through its recognition of cultural universals and the common humanity of man, helped to diminish ethnocentrism. As Kroeber has noted: "Anthropologists now agree that each culture must be examined in terms of its own structure and values, instead of being rated by the standards of some other civilization exalted as absolute — which in practice of course is always our own civilization."[29]

Kroeber has described an anthropological perspective that is generally known as the principle of cultural relativism. Herskovitz defines this principle as follows:

[25]*Ibid.,* p. 70.

[26]Paul Radin. *Primitive Religion.* New York: Dover Publications, 1957; Margaret Mead. *Sex and Temperament in Three Primitive Societies.* New York: New American Library, 1960; Franz Boas. *Primitive Art.* Irvington-on-Hudson, New York: Capitol Publishing, 1951.

[27]Herskovits, *Man and His Works, op. cit.,* p. 71.

[28]*Ibid.*

[29]Kroeber, "Anthropology," *op. cit.,* p. 87.

The principle of *cultural relativism* derives from a vast array of factual data, gained from the application of techniques in field study that have permitted us to penetrate the underlying value-systems of societies having diverse customs. This principle, briefly stated, is as follows: *Judgments are based on experience, and experience is interpreted by each individual in terms of his own enculturation.*[30]

Ruth Benedict implies agreement with this definition when she speaks of, " . . . the coexisting and equally valid patterns of life which mankind has created for itself from the raw materials of existence."[31]

Schools, as a primary source of enculturation in American society, have long been a fertile field for sowing the seeds of ethnocentrism — for fostering an "Americanization" that often neglected (and in some cases disdained) the home cultures of many students. Cultural pluralism has not often been highly valued by the public schools. Kroeber, from his vantage point as an anthropologist, shows us how foolish this has been, and contrasts it with the way in which anthropology deals with cultural pluralism:

The domain of life is certainly pluralistic, what with a million species on our own small planet. I have not heard of biologists bewailing the diversity of the species. Rather they try to find some kind of order in it. Quite correspondingly, anthropologists try to treat all cultures, including our own civilization, as parts of nature — without preferential and partisan priorities.[32]

That our schools have helped to perpetuate ethnocentrism is a sorry commentary on education in the United States. For as Solon Kimball has noted, " . . . the failure to take cultural variation into account makes some of the educational ideals and practices a farce and subverts the functions of education."[33] And, as Herskovits notes, in our perverse attempts at enculturation, we have ignored the facts that:

A final implication of the fact that culture is learned is the conclusion that *the many different ways of life that are found over the earth must each be accorded worth and dignity in its own terms*. We have seen that no logical or factual bases for the evaluation of cultures can be found, except as these are dictated by ethnocentrism. Ethnocentrism, however, is a wide-spread attitude of human groups. Men are ethnocentric either because they know no other forms of behavior than those of their own group, or if they are acquainted with the customs of foreign peoples, are driven by the force of their cultural conditioning to judge their own practices more favorably than those of another society.[34]

---

[30]Herskovits, *Man and His Works*, *op. cit.*, p. 63.

[31]Ruth Benedict. *Patterns of Culture*. Boston: Houghton Mifflin Company, 1934. p. 278.

[32]Kroeber, "Anthropology," *op. cit.*, p. 87.

[33]Solon T. Kimball. *Culture and the Educative Process*. New York: Teachers College Press, 1974. p. 81.

[34]Herskovits, *Man and His Works, op. cit.*, p. 67. (Emphasis added.)

Cultural relativism thus supports the basic concept upon which education that is multicultural is predicated: a fundamental belief that all people must be accorded *respect*, regardless of their social, ethnic, religious, and cultural backgrounds. Unless we respect and cultivate the differences among all people, and give more equal weighting to various kinds of gifts than we now do, we shall produce a deadening uniformity. Lest this seem too bold a statement, consider the fact that if you sow all the fields of an entire country with only one kind of seed, you can have a failure for the whole country of its entire crop.[35] It must be kept in mind, however, that the corrective for "white is beautiful" is not "black is beautiful." Rather, the corrective is "white — and black — and red — and yellow — are beautiful."

Discussing human diversity, Margaret Mead supports the suggestion that diversity must be respected:

When we look for the contributions which contacts of peoples, of peoples of different races and different religions, different levels of culture and different degrees of technological development, have made to education, we find two. On the one hand, the emphasis has shifted from learning to teaching, from the doing to the one who causes it to be done, from spontaneity to coercion, from freedom to power. With this shift has come the development of techniques of power, dry pedagogy, regimentation, indoctrination, manipulation and propaganda. These are but sorry additions to man's armory, and they come from the insult to human life which is perpetuated whenever one human being is regarded as differentially less or more human than another. But, on the other hand, out of the discontinuities and rapid changes which have accompanied these minglings of people has come another invention, one which perhaps would not have been born in any other setting than this one — the belief in education as an instrument for the creation of new human values.[36]

## Conclusion

Through both its recognition of the universals of experience, and its call for the respect of cultural diversity, anthropology provides undergirding for some of the basic tenets of education that is multicultural. Anthropology has "elucidated and redeveloped the concepts of culture, socialization, and social learning which are helpful in viewing the school as a culture and as part of a larger culture."[37] As a result, we are able to identify some of the shortcomings of our past educational policies and practices, and potentially to redirect

[35]Margaret Mead. "Can the Socialization of Children Lead to Greater Acceptance of Diversity?" *Young Children*. August 1973. p. 323.

[36]Margaret Mead. "Our Educational Emphases in Primitive Perspective." Nell Keddie, editor. *The Myth of Cultural Deprivation*. Harmondsworth, Middlesex, England: Penguin Books, 1973. pp. 106-107.

[37]Hilda Taba. *Curriculum Development: Theory and Practice*. New York: Harcourt Brace Jovanovich, Inc., 1962. p. 5.

our efforts toward providing a more humane, meaningful education for all children. Among these efforts, for example, would be a recognition of the distinction between language differences and linguistics, thus enabling teachers to affirm diverse languages and dialects.

Anthropology brings a perspective to education which may aid us in understanding educational processes and problems and in defining educational goals. Such a perspective can better enable us to understand the impact of culture on the school and to clarify our perceptions of the role of the school culture in shaping the lives of children. Through the application of an anthropological approach, we may view the impact of teachers' actions on the learning of values and norms, the effect of role relationships within the school culture and the society at large, and the relationship of social learning, socialization, and knowledge to the formation of student character. Such anthropological insights will be useful, for instance, in preparing and evaluating material for use in both teacher training (education) programs and the classroom. In short, anthropology can provide us with useful insights for conceptualizing, implementing, and evaluating educational programs that are multicultural.

# 5

# Why Different Education for Different Groups?

William L. Smith

A truly pluralistic society where all peoples (men and women) of the world would be viewed and appreciated for being different, for contributing, and for being equal is not reserved for the millennium. It is an achievable goal within this generation. The challenge lies in bringing it about or causing it to happen.

Specifically, in the United States, a pluralistic society is totally compatible with the nation's highest ideals. Pluralism realized would mean that all people would retain a healthy ethnic pride, an abiding sense of their own culture, and a respect for and appreciation of people and individuals from ethnically and culturally different heritages. The fact that this condition has not been realized is painfully obvious. One is often struck by the dichotomy found in certain sections of our country where people from a majority culture have positive attitudes toward an individual from another culture, but in general shun or display intolerance for the people of that culture, and in other sections manifest the opposite position, the people of another culture are accepted as a group but not as individuals. This example is but the tip of the prejudicial iceberg, but it is real — obvious and functioning enough to be destructive to human potential — in the most technologically progressive period in the history of Homo sapiens. Perhaps, unfortunately, this has been the history of civilizations throughout time. Perhaps, too, the basis for such behavior had its roots in aristocracy, patriarchy, racism, elitism, or patronage. It really does not matter.

The point is that for whatever the bias, appropriate to the time and the peoples involved, there has always been a deliberate and conscious effort to find and treat differences as a basis for inequality. Once it was called "survival of the fittest." Today it's the "haves" versus the "have nots" in both degree and kind. In a period when the technicians are able to bring time, space, distance, and peoples physically closer together, attitudes, beliefs, values, and behaviors are nevertheless keeping people further apart. Until all of us from every strata in the society can come to act and believe that to be different is still to be equal, we cannot achieve the ultimate goal of having the functioning reality of a pluralistic society.

The foregoing tenet has implications for the following question, "Does multicultural education imply different goals for different groups or individuals living in different parts of the country?" If we had achieved or begun to move toward the ultimate goal, this question would be moot. The question itself implies imperfection in our society and therefore must be viewed in an operational context either as part of a compensatory process or at least as societal remediation. Carl Grant's paper in progress entitled "Education That Is Multicultural — Isn't That What We Mean?" cites 1972 legislation enacting the Ethnic Heritage Studies Program as the first official recognition by Congress of the heterogeneous population of this country. This act proposed that people living in a multiethnic society need to have a greater understanding of their own history and the history of others.

It was not until 1972 that Congress passed a law to enable educators to deal with this critical issue in even a small way. What then has been the reality, in absence of any understanding of cultural pluralism as well as an absence of materials necessary to help children who will be leaders of our next generation or their teachers who must provide the foundation for their growth, development, and comprehension? The fact is that our society at large can be viewed as a monocultural or unicultural society which creates insensitivity. In addition many argue that the capitalistic nature of our society has only reinforced the basic bootstrap theory or the self-help, upward mobility — without institutional support — syndrome, and fosters individualism devoid of interdependence.

The fact that the state of our society is not already pluralistically ideal does not deny the extensive work being done by sociologists, anthropologists, and educators to build a knowledge base for biculturalism and multiculturalism. What has emerged as an operational dilemma is whether biculturalism and multiculturalism are means to an end — pluralism — or ends in themselves.

Grant's paper argues that a problem for educators writing about multiculturalism is that they view it as multicultural education rather than education that is multicultural. It may be inferred, as a result, that the focus is on the development of particular materials for certain people; the implication is that we have not begun to think, in the context of the whole society, of the development of materials which apply knowledge to the needs of all of the people in our society. The importance of this point is that it raises the problem of the adequacy of current approaches to defining and implementing multiculturalism in the schools.

For example, to obtain a pluralistic society, should the present concern be just for those selected groups who have not received the same kinds and numbers of societal options as did others in our society? Should the concern mean development of special kinds of materials and programs in certain parts of the United States for special groups of people? Or should the concern result in education materials being developed which will enable all people to have a greater understanding of all other people? Clearly there is a disparity between these approaches and what may be deemed appropriate to deliver on the promise.

A major problem in addressing that disparity comes from the fact that historically, in a dominant culture, many of the contributions attributed to a minority culture within that society have been ignored or treated as "nonfacts." For example, Nazi Germany, upon Adolf Hitler's rise to power in 1930-1940, had books burned, scholars imprisoned or killed, and any references to Jewish contributions to the German society, as well as to the world, deleted. History books were rewritten as if Jews never existed in Germany. Needless to say, the United States has never attempted to deny the existence of any segment of its population, whether for the odious reason that motivated Nazi Germany or for any other reason. It is nevertheless true that many individual publishers in this country, disregarding the democratic ideals of the nation, did on their own initiative exclude or disallow inclusion of significant minority culture and history in American history or civics textbooks. It was not deemed important, or in the desire to epitomize the melting pot theory, cultural differences were de-emphasized except where they had to be included as a major contribution to the history of the United States. This meant, in the case of Native Americans, that a distorted and biased view of the history was written.

This absence from written history has resulted in more anxiety, more anger, concern, and frustration on the parts of people from those particular minority cultures affected whether black, brown, yellow, or red. The unabridged United States history is in many instances painful to remember, but is part of what has honed, tempered, and matured members of minority groups. Euro-Americans, too, have affinity with the black, yellow, red, and brown Americans, although often they have forgotten their gaunt years of long ago. They, too, were persecuted once because they spoke a strange tongue, celebrated a different Sabbath, or ate foods with strange odors. To escape from or deny the tribal heritage of the ethnic majority is equally as unjust as excluding the cultural heritage of the ethnic minority.

Barbara Sizemore presents a comprehensive analysis of a five-stage power-inclusion model that she says each of the Euro-American tribes went through, and which excluded minority groups must go through to achieve group mobility and full citizenship in the American social order before this society can seriously address a culturally pluralistic reality.

First is the ongoing separatist stage process during which the excluded group defines its identity. Second is the nationalist stage in which the excluded group intensifies its cohesion by building a religio-cultural community of beliefs around its own creation, history, and development, which in most instances causes the rejection of the social order of others. Third is the capitalistic stage during which the group cohesion developed in the separatist and nationalist periods produces an awareness of the need that makes it possible to build an economic base for the minority group. Fourth is the pluralistic stage when the group utilizes its cohesion-rejection powers and its economic base to form a political bloc to thrust its interests into the foreground of the political arena. Fifth is the egalitarian or democratic stage in which the interests of the group have just as much chance as other groups at this level of participation. Sizemore sees this as utopian in the American social order. There is a sixth stage not addressed by Sizemore which may come even closer to utopia. It is the independence with interdependence stage. All ethnic, racial, and tribal groups make a reentry into their own ethnicity, not for protection but for the enhancement of self-worth, self-respect, and identity and competence. The position we are seeking has to do with the most fundamental element in human well-being. When a man or woman has answered the ontological questions — where I came from, who I am, and where I am going — the movement forward to share with others and to learn of and help meet their needs will be accomplished earnestly and eagerly.

Culture and heritage studies will grow out of introspection engaged in by curriculum designers, teachers, and ultimately children. Introspection linked with objective historical research and scholarship provide a sound basis for materials to be written thoroughly and frankly. It is my personal opinion that members of the minority or majority subject group can and should validate materials so that subtle prejudices can be screened from the work. Out of this would come a revised common core of values, common to each nationality in this nation. Teachers would be able to come to know and accept themselves, the multiethnic or multiracial materials they use, and the children with whom they work and whom they influence. To be independent with interdependence requires a sense of confidence and security in a complex social system. It will bring about a new sense of being and of wholeness in the entire society through a strengthening of its parts.

Alex Haley, the author of *Roots*, has had his book adapted for television in the same manner as Irwin Shaw's book *Rich Man, Poor Man*. The adaptation was broadcast in January 1977. His 12 years of researching and writing *Roots* have provided him with insights which are applicable to our discussion. His belief is that all people from every ethnicity and race should do two things: (a) Encourage the oldest persons in the family to share the oral history passed down from generation to generation. Go up to attics and down to basements and gather, organize, and use all of those old papers, pictures, and materials that have been saved, passed, or preserved over the years from generation to generation. (b) Encourage more and more family reunions so that all ages can come together to learn and share. All will leave a little richer than when they arrived.

How simple and yet how important is his proposal to the concept of independence with interdependence. What better way to begin the process of answering the ontological questions, to build a renewed sense of self, to commence the process of sharing — first within and then without.

To go back to the question asked in this paper about different goals for different groups, it seems abundantly clear to this author that each of the stages in the development of groups toward their full participation in society is a means toward that end. Even if these stages in contemporary American society are not exactly as Sizemore has described, minority groups are at different places in such stages of development, and until each has moved to a comparable level, I believe that it will be wise and necessary to develop knowledge and materials specific to the needs of each group to ensure the authenticity of their own culture and heritage. But this must always be approached on the means-end continuum. The process must be designed so as to accomplish what I consider to be the ultimate goal: awakening our society to the reality and goodness of a culturally pluralistic curriculum which will accurately represent our diverse society. If we are successful the next generation of Americans will live the ideal that to be different is not to be inferior — to be different is to be equal. Even more important, they will live the ideal that being different doesn't matter.

Within our sprawling and seemingly impersonal society there is a chronic need to know, spiritually and rationally, the worth of the individual. We must develop individuals who are open to change, who are flexible and receptive and adaptive. This means introducing them to a variety of life-styles, in-depth and not superficially. Students of all races must study the richness of America's multicultural and multiracial heritage. Only then will we be able to say and mean "education that is multicultural" rather than "multicultural-multiracial education."

# 6

# Is Multicultural Education a New Attempt at Acculturation?

**William M. Newman**

"Is multicultural education truly preserving pluralism, or is it a smoke-screen for a new attempt at acculturation?" This question is difficult to answer because, like most questions about social policies, it contains a number of unexamined assumptions. In this case it is assumed that we have precise knowledge about previous educational policies and their effects upon ethnic groups in the United States. It is also implied that the current revival of ethnic consciousness and its consequences for educational institutions are fully understood. Finally, the question assumes that multicultural education programs are here to stay, and that the only salient issue is whether these programs will promote or undermine pluralistic understandings of the American social structure. I find it difficult to agree with these several assumptions. In fact, an examination of these assumptions is a necessary route to providing a realistic answer to the question that has been posed.

## Historical Considerations

An accurate grasp of the meaning of the history of American educational policies is essential to any assessment of the present situation. There appears to be firm evidence that during the colonial period formal educational training was intended to preserve the different religio-ethnic cultures that existed in the different colonies and later states.[1] Yet, dramatic changes occurred in both American society and in education during the 19th century. As I have tried to suggest in *American Pluralism,*[2] American society was transformed from a structure of segregated pluralism to one of integrated pluralism. As a result of the combined effects of massive immigration, urbanization, and industrialism, the pattern of religio-ethnic segregation on a broad geographic scale disintegrated. In its place emerged a form of integrated pluralism, in which most locales exhibited a microcosm of diversity, composed of peoples from different cultures interacting with each other in the public spheres on a daily basis.

It is only in the context of a structure of segregated pluralism that many of the institutional features of early American history make sense. For instance, the constitutional protection of religious freedom was really intended to protect the segregated turfs of the different religio-ethnic communities in the separate colonies. It was designed to protect Congregationalism in New England, the culture of Quakerism in Pennsylvania, and Catholicism in Maryland. These basically conservative impulses dominated educational policies during the early years of the republic as well. As Tewkesbury has shown, conservative and protectionist attitudes in the form of denominational competition were an essential element in the rapid emergence of higher educational institutions prior to the mid-19th century.[3] The important point, though, is that these patterns in American society and in American educational institutions underwent dramatic change. The important questions are when did these changes occur and what were their effects?

It is ironic that even after America's bicentennial, the colonial period is perhaps the only era for which there is even a semblance of unanimity of interpretation among historians. In my view, the triple forces of immigration, urbanization, and industrialization that set the context for contemporary educational policies began to make their impact in the last quarter of the 19th century. Yet, historians such as Richard Brown argue convincingly that a new structural and cultural situation had already emerged by the 1830's, and that the crescendo of the Civil War blinds our perception of the modernization and homogenization of American society well before mid-century.[4] It is at least agreed that by the mid-19th century an important new

[1]Bernard Bailyn. *Education in the Forming of American Society*. Chapel Hill, North Carolina: University of North Carolina Press, 1960. pp. 100-106.

[2]William M. Newman. *American Pluralism: A Study of Minority Groups and Social Theory*. New York: Harper & Row, Publishers, 1973. pp. 53-63.

[3]Donald G. Tewkesbury. *The Founding of American Colleges and Universities Before the Civil War*. Ph.D. dissertation. New York: Columbia University, 1932.

[4]Richard Brown. "Modernization and Modern Personality in Early America, 1600-1865: A Sketch of a Synthesis." *Journal of Interdisciplinary History* 2: 201-88; Winter 1972.

concept, that of free public education, was already making its impact upon American society and the immigrants entering it.

The standard textbook interpretation is that free public education quickly became the assimilative glue for integrating a society of increasingly diverse peoples. It is argued that the common or public schools acculturated the immigrants, trained them for roles in the scheme of industrial capitalism, and generally served as a mechanism of social mobility for ethnic groups.[5] However, within the last decade a revisionist school of educational historians has provided quite a different picture of things. Here it is argued that textbooks and the day-to-day operations of the schools were designed to depict the immigrants as different and inferior;[6] that to the extent that public schools trained ethnics for industrial jobs, the effect was to prevent them from experiencing social mobility;[7] and most importantly, educational attainment for ethnics followed social mobility rather than causing it.[8]

These two radically different pictures of the meaning of public education for ethnic groups are both correct, though in different ways. It is true that assimilation and social mobility were the advertised purposes of public education. It is also true that educational practices thwarted both of these things for immigrant groups. In other words, there has been a conflict between ideology and practice in public education. The situation is basically like that described by Myrdal in *An American Dilemma,* in which he contends that while American society advertised the ideology of individual freedom and equal opportunity, social practices were designed to retard and restrain the advancement of American blacks.[9] While there are important differences between the experiences of the so-called new minorities (blacks, Puerto Ricans, Chicanos) and white ethnics, the basic scenario is the same.

Thus, the question whether multicultural education really is "a new attempt at acculturation" misses the crucial point that there probably never were any real attempts at acculturation. The standard textbook view that public education was designed to promote assimilation ignores an enormous conflict between ideology and practice in American public education. While ethnics of all kinds have been told that the public schools would make them assimilated, socially mobile participants in American society, everything has

---

[5]Lawrence Cremin. *The Genius of American Education*. New York: Vintage Press, 1966.

[6]Colin Greer. *The Great School Legend: A Revisionist Interpretation of American Public Education*. New York: Basic Books, 1972.

[7]Joel H. Spring. *Education and the Rise of the Corporate State*. Boston: Beacon Press, 1972; and Elizabeth and Michael Useem, editors. *The Educational Establishment*. Englewood Cliffs, New Jersey: Prentice-Hall, Inc., 1974.

[8]David K. Cohen. "Immigrants and the Schools." *Review of Educational Research* 40:12-27; February 1970.

[9]Gunnar Myrdal. *An American Dilemma*. New York: Harper & Row, Publishers, 1944.

been done in educational institutions (as elsewhere) to prevent these things from happening.

## The Revival of Ethnic Consciousness

Given that the traditions in American public education regarding ethnic groups that developed in the late 19th century were fraught with paradox and conflict, how has the contemporary revival of ethnic consciousness affected these traditions? I am inclined to think that the ethnic revival will have relatively little lasting impact upon our educational institutions. This is because the revival of ethnicity in the 1970's is basically a socially and politically conservative, rather than liberal, movement.

As I have suggested elsewhere,[10] both class and status conflicts were the motor forces behind the emergence of what some are calling the "new pluralism." The successive demands for a share of the resources of American society made by blacks, Spanish-speaking Americans, women's liberation, and similar movements finally, under the strains of a dwindling economy, resulted in a backlash among the white ethnics. Though the census figures for the period 1960-1970 show that the black-white income gap had become greater, both a depressed economy and the media coverage given the various emerging minority movements convinced white ethnics that their star was falling in terms of both wealth and social prestige. The revival of ethnic consciousness was far from a liberal humanitarian movement created in the name of pluralistic human dignity. Rather, it was born of relative deprivation, based in essence on a "we want ours too" perception.

As most of the great classical period writers in sociology have shown, there need not be any rational connection between the origins of a social movement and the consequences it has for a society. It is possible that an ethnic revival born of perceived class and status deprivations may unintentionally result in more enlightened policies and practices. The efforts of individual ethnic groups to promote their own interests may result in compromises that work toward common interests. It is possible, for instance, that one result of the ethnic revival will be that ethnics no longer need to apologize for being ethnic. While this does not mean that educational practices will automatically shift to a genuine emphasis on social pluralism, it may mean that the traditional myth of assimilation and of education's role in it will be abandoned. Yet, it is a luxury to talk in terms of generalities when in fact we have a specific range of multicultural educational programs that are being initiated

---

[10]William M. Newman. "A Revival of Ethnic Consciousness: A Look At America's Rediscovered Pluralism." *Journal of Current Social Issues* 10:12-18; 1972.

and that concern us. Let me turn then to an assessment of these programs in the context of the themes that I have developed here.

## Educational Issues and Probabilities

Regardless of which level of the educational system is examined, from the elementary school to the state university, certain basic policy positions or strategies for implementing multiculturalism in education appear to dominate the debate. From the present vantage point there are at least three issues upon which multiculturalism will either stand or fall. These are, the principle of pluralism in educational staffing, the principle of multilingualism, and the matter of curriculum reform and innovation. In other words, most educational policy and program debates center around the questions of whether these principles are desirable, whether they are likely to be implemented, and what their consequences are likely to be.

I suspect that most people agree in principle with the idea that educational staffs, given the availability of qualified personnel, ought to reflect the social and cultural pluralism of the social structure. However, the basic mechanism for implementing this ideal, quota systems, is highly controversial. Even in American history, quota systems, both formal and informal, have been used to both restrict and create opportunity for members of different groups. Opponents of quota systems in education argue that these techniques ultimately restrict opportunity and create as closed a system as they are designed to eliminate. It is argued that racial and ethnic quotas contradict the basic ideal of freedom of opportunity for all who will work hard and take advantage of the opportunities that exist. Obviously, proponents of hiring quotas respond that if the system really worked that way we would not need quotas. Therefore, we should opt for quotas as the lesser of two evils.

The experience of the 1970's, in terms of already established government equal employment regulations, suggests that the sheer bureaucracy needed to implement formal quotas has moved otherwise sympathetic supporters to circumvent them where possible. I suspect that an outright system of quotas will encourage minorities to fight with each other rather than work together for reasonable reform in hiring practices. One can only hope that moderate techniques will be found that will really create greater minority representation on educational staffs. If it is recalled that historically we have experienced a conflict in ideology and practice in education, it stands to reason that increased pluralism in educational staffs will change day-to-day operations in education. The ultimate result can be a genuine reflection of pluralistic values in education. This will surely take time to occur, and the outcome clearly rests upon our ability to find techniques for the integration of educational staffs that avoid the negative consequences of rigid and competitive quota formulas.

The question of multilingualism is a more difficult one to address. In the United States we have not had a formal tradition of multilingualism, nor have we had a tradition of politicizing ethnic differences to the point that all ethnic relations must be governed by legalistic techniques. To see the negative consequences of such an approach one need only look at the volatile debates that are today tearing apart Canadian society.[11] I can only state my own value preferences on the basis of my own understanding of how American society works, when it works. As I have suggested elsewhere American society contains processes that pull toward assimilation and pluralism at the same time.[12] It is clear that the public sectors of American society, especially its economy and politics, rest upon the assumption of a common core culture. Traditionally, people who have wished to partake in the American feast in some way have learned to participate in that Americanized mainstream. To say this is not to deny the legitimacy of voluntary segregation or the maintenance of strong subcultures. While there are important instances of voluntary residential and cultural separatism in the United States, relatively few groups have been able to remain entirely outside mainstream political and economic channels.

Translated into educational policies, I am saying that parallel track linguistic education would be a mistake. Ultimately, like the Canadian example, it results in political battles over which of the many will get to be the lingua francae or cultura francae. There can be dignity and value in offering and preserving multilingual skills in the American population. This is one of the few modern nation-states in which such a high degree of monolingualism exists. English as a Second Language programs are useful and important. But I think that regardless of how much we are able to preserve diverse cultures and languages, the American educational system should equip minorities to participate in the cultural mainstream where the material rewards are being distributed. While much of what I have said on this issue reflects value judgments, scientifically I cannot easily predict a radical departure from our traditions on this issue. Moreover, I am convinced that both assimilationists and pluralists must recognize the degree to which both processes exist in American society. To see the inevitability of political and economic assimilation is not to deny the legitimacy of the existence of subcultures alongside it. Educating for both sets of institutional arrangements is a difficult task.

Whether curriculum reform and innovation will foster authentically

---

[11]John Porter. "Ethnic Pluralism in Canadian Perspective." Nathan Glazer and Daniel P. Moynihan, editors. *Ethnicity: Theory and Practice*. Cambridge, Massachusetts: Harvard University Press, 1975. pp. 267-304.

[12]William M. Newman, *American Pluralism, op. cit.*

pluralistic values is more easily answered. There are two primary retarding factors. The first, personnel, has already been discussed. So long as public schools are controlled and staffed by people who are not in sympathy with a pluralistic ideology, pluralism will not be taught. Even the best curriculum materials can be used in ways that thwart the stated goals of these materials. Assuming that we have the human resources to create curriculum materials that tell the American story in a pluralistic way, the second major retarding factor is funding. Funding is required to create teaching materials and to allow public schools to purchase them.

Frankly, I am somewhat pessimistic about the speed at which these things will happen. The present economic conditions in the United States have put extreme pressures on public school financing at the local, state, and federal levels. Government has not made a financial commitment to allow educational institutions to correct the abuses of the past regarding ethnic groups.

In summary, I believe that the historical record is not an encouraging one, and I am not convinced that the present ethnic revival will create lasting changes in the educational system. Some combination of new staffing arrangements and curriculum development can open the school doors to a genuinely pluralistic understanding of American society. Since I don't believe that the public schools ever really attempted to acculturate the immigrants, I have little fear that present multicultural education efforts are actually a smokescreen for more of the same. The real danger is that multicultural education programs will simply fall by the wayside because of lack of political support and funding. If this happens, we will simply be left with the traditional paradoxes in education between what we say and what we do about the question of ethnic pluralism in American society.

# 7

# Language Instruction and Multicultural Education

Muriel Saville-Troike

Language is an inescapable aspect of multicultural education. Multiple cultures entail multiple linguistic codes, and the codes serve the essential function of transmitting cultural information and values from one generation to the next, whether at home or at school, within or across groups. Furthermore, the language forms which people use are inexorably tied to their group and individual identity, to their attitudes toward others, and to their communicative effectiveness in the various social domains in which they may need or wish to function.

A number of issues in this area are still far from resolved, and the decisions which must be made with respect to these issues will have to take into account social, political, and economic as well as linguistic and educational factors. Precisely because language is so closely bound with people's identities, attitudes, and opportunities, members of the diverse social groups represented in multicultural contexts are justifiably demanding participation in this realm of education.

With specific regard to the relationship of language instruction to multicultural education, a number of very basic questions remain. The most important is whether the cognitive and affective goals of multicultural education can be achieved if the monolingual code of standard school English is the sole mode for their transmission and expression; or whether such programs must provide for multilingualism as well, or even promote it, if they are to be successful.

When the educational context is one in which students understand little or no English, this question has essentially already been decided by laws and decrees;[1] students who cannot understand the language of instruction clearly cannot learn effectively, and instruction or support in their native language is widely accepted as necessary if they are to have equal opportunity for education.[2] The appropriate role of students' native language is still an issue in educational contexts in which students are from culturally diverse backgrounds, but all understand English (though many may speak varieties of the language considered "nonstandard" in the school context). Also at question is whether a multilingual component is necessary or useful in a situation in which students and teachers are from a fairly homogeneous linguistic and cultural background and are learning about other groups in a program of multicultural education.

In terms of curriculum and classroom practices, recognizing the linguistic dimension of multicultural education can mean three quite different procedures, depending on program goals and the linguistic and cultural composition of the students involved. First, when students are members of the cultural groups being studied, and goals include enhancing the self-concept, cultural confidence, and communicative effectiveness of minority group members within their own community, multilingual instruction can mean using students' own linguistic codes as media of teaching, learning, and expression. Second, with the same students and goals, multilingual considerations can rather be realized as the acceptance and encouragement of students' native language codes in learning and self-expression, but the exclusive use of standard school English in instruction. Finally, especially in contexts in which students are a relatively homogeneous group of mainstream speakers of standard English learning about "others" in their society, and program goals include developing cultural relativism, respect for others, and appreciation and acceptance of cultural variety, multilingual considerations can be realized by teaching about other language systems in a positive light, by including recordings, speakers, and texts which expose students to other linguistic codes in functional communicative contexts, and which teach understanding of language systems other than their own in relation to whatever other cognitive and affective concepts about the cultures are being transmitted.

Although the goals stated above which are associated with the first mode of

[1]Hannah N. Geffert, Robert J. Harper II, Salvador Sarmiento, and Daniel M. Schember. *The Current Status of U.S. Bilingual Education Legislation.* Arlington, Virginia: Center for Applied Linguistics, 1975.

[2]Statements of this position occur in a number of sources, including a publication by the United States Commission on Civil Rights. *A Better Chance To Learn: Bilingual-Bicultural Education.* Publication 51. Washington, D.C.: U.S. Government Printing Office, May 1975.

relating a multilingual component to multicultural education (enhancing the self-concept, cultural confidence, and communicative effectiveness of minority group students) may sound unassailable to proponents of such programs, there are economic and political implications on both sides which should be considered. To begin with, making use of students' linguistic codes for instruction entails that teachers also be bilingual or bidialectal — a boon in terms of increased job opportunities for minority-group teachers, but a clear threat to the present and future educators who by heritage or choice can communicate only in a mainstream variety of standard English. Also in the economic realm is the possible eligibility of such multilingual programs (including those utilizing nonstandard varieties of English) for the substantial sources of federal and state funding now being allotted bilingual education, versus the strong resistance which might be expected from the other language groups now receiving all such funds.

Along political dimensions, the most serious questions concern the importance of a common language code to a common American identity, or the desirability and feasibility of encouraging the maintenance of separate languages and cultures in the United States. Opponents of multilingual education fear a divisive potential and a strengthening of ethnic and racial boundaries, while proponents either argue for the value of self and family identity over national identity or the better adjusted national group membership which may follow establishment of positive self and cultural concepts.[3] Closely related is the sensitive issue of integration, for bilingual or multilingual programs which feature instruction in languages other than standard English are typically composed almost entirely of students from a single cultural group. This might well be considered a form of de facto segregation.

The second mode of relating a multilingual component to multicultural education (accepting the use of students' native language codes but not teaching in them) resolves some of these problems, but raises others. While the teacher need not be a speaker of the students' language or dialect, the need is also eliminated for the teacher to provide a positive role model for minority group students and to demonstrate true acceptance of their language through its use. The teacher in this case is providing a model for standard English, however, and in a way which allows students some choice in their own language use and cultural identity. The underlying rationale of most proponents of this mode is that students who speak nonstandard varieties of English should be given the opportunity to acquire standard English in order to be able to communicate effectively in a wider range of social contexts

[3]Wallace E. Lambert. "Culture and Language as Factors in Learning and Education." Paper presented at the convention of Teachers of English to Speakers of Other Languages. Denver, Colorado, March 1974.

and have access to a wider range of economic and educational opportunities. The phrase "should be given the opportunity" is the key here, implying that if school instruction is not in standard English, many students will not have such an opportunity, and will thus have limited access to many occupations and to higher education. This is probably the majority view among parents of students who learn nonstandard English at home and in their communities; but some reject it as imperialistic and not really offering a choice, and some want their children to be *forced* in some way to use standard English at school.

The third mode, teaching about other language varieties without using them, generates least controversy, either because it is a more conservative step into multilingual-multicultural education, or because the dominant group which generally composes such classes has less at stake as a result of the instruction. Whether or not these students develop an appreciation for and acceptance of linguistic and cultural diversity will not appreciably affect their own economic and political opportunity or security — only that of the "others" they are studying. The few strong community proponents are those that place a high value on the development of humanistic concepts in their children, and the few opponents are likely to consider it a waste of time which should be spent teaching the 3 R's.

To give primary attention to the social, political, and economic issues which influence decisions about adding some type of multilingual component to multicultural education is not to imply that more scholarly issues are not also involved. Educators, linguists, psychologists, and anthropologists all consider this topic within their professional domain, and all have relevant insights and hypotheses to bring to bear on it.

Educators accept as axiomatic that instruction should begin where the students are, and an understanding of what this entails when those students are from linguistically and culturally diverse backgrounds is critical for any discussion of the role of language in multicultural education. This axiom is often interpreted to mean that remediation should be provided for the "disadvantaged" students so that they will have the same background as the "advantaged" ones, that is, those of the dominant culture. Implementation of this viewpoint often involves finding the lowest common linguistic and conceptual denominator among students, teacher, and available instructional material, and considering that level appropriate for instruction. An alternative interpretation is to begin from what the students *do* know rather than what they do *not* know about the mainstream culture. Not giving credit for what is known builds a deficit model into the whole process, and controls many of the perceptions and expectations of both teachers and the students themselves. All children come to school with a background of many experiences, with already established attitudes, values, and beliefs, with conceptual development well under way, and with the ability to understand and express themselves in at least one linguistic code already acquired. To fail to utilize and build upon the knowledge and skills students have already learned is surely not beginning instruction where they are. An even greater violation of this axiom occurs, however, in many cases where prior learning is recognized but not accepted; if it does not happen to be the language and culture of the school, it may be considered less than nothing — a handicap to further education.

The importance of continuity in learning between home and school and the value of using the students' language to allow uninterrupted cognitive development have been widely recognized in the rapid spread and acceptance of bilingual education, but only if the students' language is not English at all. That language-related learning problems may also be encountered by students who speak a nonstandard variety of English is clearly documented by the Commission on Civil Rights, which reports even lower reading achievement for black students than for speakers of Spanish, Chinese, or Native American languages.[4] Similar differential achievement results are commonly reported in all content areas closely associated with language, which include science and social studies, as well as reading, spelling, and others classified as language arts.

The learning problems of speakers of nonstandard English are clearly very different from those of speakers of other languages, and undoubtedly much more closely related to inappropriate classroom practices and to attitudinal factors than to the linguistic differences per se, although these causes are often unrecognized. A common example of inappropriate reading instruction occurs when a student reads a sentence such as *They are walking fast* as "Dey walkin' fas'" and is corrected word by word on pronunciation and grammar, even though the written form has been accurately encoded into the student's linguistic system. By not accepting the student's language in this reading context, the teacher inhibits fluency and ultimately discourages reading itself. Similar examples can be drawn from any classroom situation which requires students to respond orally, or to encode or decode their spoken language in writing or reading. Not only does the teacher make corrections of language forms which are not relevant to the cognitive task at hand, but the misunderstanding of linguistic differences triggers stereotyping, which in turn controls attitudes, expectations, and much subsequent interaction, even with other students in the class.

One possible answer to this problem is accepting each student's language, and teaching respect and acceptance of language variety to other students as well. Further, linguistic differences can be recognized in such aspects of

[4]United States Commission on Civil Rights. *The Unfinished Education*. Report 2 of the Mexican American Educational Series. Washington, D.C.: U.S. Government Printing Office, October 1971.

instruction as teaching sound-symbol correspondences or spelling rules, truly beginning where the student is in a positive way: multilingual education.

An issue which arises at this point, often addressed from or to linguists, is the potential effect of allowing nonstandard English at school: does it lead to decline of the language or the use of language? After all, isn't a major purpose of school to teach educated English?

To begin with, most linguists feel educators vastly overrate the influence of school on language development. Basic patterns of pronunciation and grammar have already been largely established before a child comes to school, and students continue to find most of their language models outside of the classroom. Especially as students approach adolescence, peers have much more linguistic influence on their language usage than do teachers or books. This has been proven by research which shows that black adolescents in inner city schools use more nonstandard forms than do younger students in the same areas, in spite of the fact that the adolescents have had more years of formal English instruction and more exposure to the language models which teachers provide.[5]

Few linguists would argue that standard English should not be taught, but most would agree that nonstandard varieties (just as other languages) are equally valid as vehicles for learning and self-expression. The learning barrier for speakers of nonstandard English is not primarily linguistic, but social and attitudinal in nature. People are judged, typed, and classified by the variety of language they speak. Internal classification (group identity) is also partly based on language, which is why the standard language models of school are often rejected by adolescents to whom peer group identity is more highly valued.

While remembering the differences between learning another language and learning another variety of the same language, part of the rationale and methodology for bilingual education may be applied to bidialectal education as well. In that model, initial expression and instruction is in the native linguistic code of the students, with standard English added as a second language system. It is important for attitudinal as well as cognitive reasons that no effort is made to eradicate the first language, but to add a second in order to extend the range of contexts in which the students may communicate effectively. Acquiring standard English is of recognized importance in this society, but that goal may come to much more widespread realization if its implementation does not require students to reject their family and peer identity in the process. Additionally, other language-related learning problems may well be alleviated when attitudinal and pedagogical barriers have been lowered.

[5]Contributions to such research have most notably been made by William Labov and Walter Loban.

Some psychologists disagree with linguists on the value of a multilingual approach to education, saying that "disadvantaged" students should not be presented with too many choices, or they will become confused. Counter evidence also comes from psychologists, however, who suggest that learning more than one linguistic code may increase cognitive flexibility, a recognized measure of intelligence.[6] It is difficult to draw any conclusions about the relation of language learning and use to intelligence because of the inherent linguistic and cultural biases of tests used to make such evaluations, and conclusions which have been drawn should be viewed with suspicion. The fact that in one recently integrated school district over half of the black students were assigned to classes for the mentally retarded says nothing about these students' intellectual capacity; it says rather that the misunderstanding and misdiagnosis of linguistic and cultural differences are preventing hundreds of students from having equal educational opportunities.

Most attention has been given thus far in this discussion to the role of language in the education of black students who speak a nonstandard variety of English because this group seems most handicapped at present by programs and teachers that do not understand or respect the validity of their linguistic systems. Also included in terms of the role of language in multicultural education, however, are students who are speakers of other languages, students who are speakers of other varieties of English that differ from the language of their school, and students (from many ethnic and racial backgrounds) who speak a mainstream variety of standard English. It is to the general role of language in multicultural education for *all* students that anthropologists most directly relate, for they show us that language is an integral and inseparable part of culture, just as religion, family structure, and shared heritage are part of culture. Attempting to teach about cultures without taking their linguistic component into account is to ignore a critical dimension of their expression and identity.

The social, political, and economic questions raised above about the desirability of multilingual education are thus essentially questions about the desirability of multicultural education as a whole, or of the degree to which the objectives of multicultural education are considered worthwhile. A parent or teacher who feels multilingualism is potentially divisive will also feel that recognizing and accepting diverse values, beliefs, and social identities is a threat to national unity. A parent or teacher who values cultural pluralism and considers it a resource to be respected and cultivated in education will also respect the linguistic variety which reflects and expresses it.

The role of language in multicultural education is thus an absolutely

[6]Wallace E. Lambert, "Culture and Language as Factors in Learning and Education," *op. cit.*

essential one unless programs are to be at the surface level of tasting ethnic foods, breaking piñatas at Christmas, and hanging posters obtained from a travel agent. Even more important, understanding and accepting linguistic diversity is critical for all aspects of instruction for students from diverse cultural backgrounds if they are to have an opportunity to achieve their full potential within our educational system.

# 8

# Sexism and Language: Two Dimensions

Susan L. Melnick

Consideration of sexist bias in American society often leads to the English language, in which sexism is reflected and perpetuated. Although a number of research studies and discussions of sexist bias in the English language are available, the majority of Americans might not be as aware of sexist bias as they should be. While education that is multicultural demands recognition of the wide diversity of languages spoken in our society, an examination of sexism in English is an initial step to exposing discrimination against women inherent in many languages. This discussion considers an overview of significant topics in the area and of alternatives we might implement for schooling and for society in general.

## Sex Differentiation in Language

Clearly, the American male and female occupy different sex statuses. They are predisposed by behavioral orientation toward different experiences. As a medium of expression of one's experiences, language reflects these differences, both in use and form. More than a means of communication for one's experiences, language is also an expression of shared assumptions. Therefore, language transmits implicit values and behavioral models to all members of a speech community.[1] Our identities — who and what we are and

[1]E. Burr, S. Dunn, and N. Farquhar. "Women and the Language of Inequality." *Social Education* 36: 841-45; 1972.

think we are, how others see and define us — are greatly affected by this differential use of language. As Whorf noted:

The background linguistic system of each language is not merely a reproducing instrument for voicing ideas, but rather is itself a shaper of ideas, the program and guide for the individual's mental activity, for his [sic] analysis of impressions for his [sic] synthesis of his [sic] mental stock in trade.[2]

Because humans order and interpret reality through symbols, language is both the reflector and formulator of cultural expectations.

In this dual role of cultural transmission, the English language reflects a history, a world view, an understanding of one another, and the value people place on their lives together. In the past decade, however, it has become increasingly clear that this cultural view which the language transmits is characterized primarily by the dominant value system in American society. Recent linguistic investigations reveal numerous instances of sexist bias, both reflected and formulated by the language we use. This bias is apparent in two major dimensions of linguistic discrimination against women: (a) Male dominance, reflected in general linguistic use, which treats women as objects and appendages, as a subculture of the male; and (b) sex differences in language use, determined by psycholinguistic analyses, which characterize "women's language" as different (and presumably deficient) from that of men. These two dimensions merit careful scrutiny because they perpetuate the stereotypes "that have been so completely woven into the cultural fabric that they have become a habit of traditional thinking and perception [and are] regarded as the only habit of truth."[3] These stereotyped linguistic habits should be understood as images that tend more to socialize our thinking than to reflect inherent traits of women and men.

Here, all instances of male dominance and/or differential patterning will be considered sexist language, defined as any language that expresses stereotyped attitudes and expectations or assumes the inherent superiority of one sex over the other.[4] Attention will be given to male dominance, primarily as revealed by research studies on vocabulary; the dimension of sex differences will be discussed primarily in terms of research studies investigating the quality and quantity of language spoken by women.

[2]H.S. O'Donnell. "Sexism in Language." *Elementary English* 50: 1067; 1973.

[3]H.L. Gershuny. "Sexist Semantics in the Dictionary." *ETC: A Review of General Semantics* 31: 159; 1973.

[4]C. Miller and K. Swift. "One Small Step for Genkind." *The New York Times Magazine.* April 16, 1972, p. 36.

## Male Dominance

As early as 1922, Otto Jespersen characterized the English language as "positively and expressly masculine. . . . It is the language of a grown-up man and has very little childish or feminine about it."[5] Despite the increased sophistication of linguistic study during the past 50 years, this language of male dominance persists. Even the definitions of "woman" and "man" support this fact: According to the *Oxford English Dictionary*, considered as the most authoritative dictionary of the English language, "woman" is defined as (1) an adult female being; (2) a female servant; (3) a lady-love or mistress; (4) a wife. "Man," however, is defined as (1) a human being; (2) a human creature regarded abstractly; (3) an adult male creature endowed with manly qualities; (4) a person of position and importance.[6] These connotations not only respond to society's attitudes but also perpetuate these same notions which keep women in subordinate positions.

Dictionaries such as the *OED* have traditionally been accorded the role of cultural authorities of meaning and usage. In a study designed to determine the extent to which the *Random House Dictionary*, for example, acts as a doctrinaire expert to reinforce and legitimatize sex role stereotypes, Gershuny found that, in a sample of 2,000 illustrative sentences selected from 900 entry words, masculine-gender sentence contexts outnumber feminine-gender contexts 3:1; masculine words outnumber feminine words 2:1.[7] Despite the inherent neutrality of such words as "bargain," "trembled," "fire," and "nerves," Gershuny found that the illustrative sentences invested the words not only with specific meaning but with a biased authenticity, authority, and stability merely because they appeared in the dictionary: "His mother-in-law was no *bargain*; she *trembled* at his voice; he said he would go through *fire* and water to win her hand; women with shrill voices get on his *nerves*." These qualitative findings confirm what Varda One terms the "mythos of lexicographic objectivity"[8] of the dictionary, while the quantitative results suggest the relative unimportance of the feminine gender in defining and being defined in English. In spite of other efforts, such as Houghton-Mifflin's $5 million study to determine and remediate dictionary bias,[9] sexism in language is still manifested in (a) the vocabulary of the language, either by denotation or connotation, and (b) in the language structure, especially by pronouns and suffixes.

[5]O. Jespersen. *Growth and Structure of the English Language*. Oxford: Basil Blackwell, 1935. p. 2.

[6]O'Donnell, "Sexism in Language," *op. cit.*, p. 1067.

[7]Gershuny, "Sexist Semantics in the Dictionary," *op. cit.*, p. 166.

[8]Varda One. *Manglish*. Pittsburgh, Pennsylvania: KNOW, Inc., 1971.

[9]F.D. Rhome. "Manglish: What's It All About?" Paper presented at the meeting of the Midwest Modern Language Association. St. Louis, Missouri, 1972.

The vocabulary of the language is the set of individual words we use in communication. As Morton notes, however, words do more than signify:

> They conjure images . . . which rise out of the conscious and unconscious lives individually and in community that shape styles of life long before conceptualization takes place.[10]

Equally as odious as derogatory ethnic terms, yet more subtle, are the images created in the mind by words regarded as "respectable." For example, the counterparts steward/stewardess, bachelor/spinster, and master/mistress, while ostensibly respectful, conjure images of women in subordinate positions, occupationally and socially. This type of biased imagery has been documented in numerous studies and discussions,[11] which arrive at similar conclusions: Women are, by and large, viewed as either appendages or objects, and their position is, without exception, subordinate to the male's. The following examples are but a few of the many occurrences found in daily use:

1. *Academic referent.* Bachelor of arts and master of arts degrees are linguistically masculine, orginally named in expectation of male-only achievement. In spite of the large number of women enrolled in institutions of higher education, scholarship holders continue to be termed *fellows* and first year students, *freshmen.*[12]

2. *Semantic discrepancy.* Although such counterparts as landlord/landlady and courtier/courtesan derived from a common origin, the revolutionary process of words involving women indicates that the female form moves in a degrading direction. For example, courtier/courtesan orginally meant "fawning behavior"; the current meaning for the male form is "flatterer," while the female form means "prostitute." Words such as *wench* and *harlot*, which used to mean "weakling" and "camp follower" respectively, were originally used to signify both female and male. Their use since the 16th century, however, is restricted to women and the meanings carry degrading sexual connotations.[13]

---

[10]N. Morton. "The Rising Woman Consciousness in a Male Language Structure." *Andover Newton Quarterly* 12: 177; 1972.

[11]R. Lakoff. "Language and Woman's Place." *Language in Society* 2: 45-79; 1973; A. Nilsen and D. Nilsen. "Mr. and Mrs. Nilsen Debate Sexism in English." Workshop presented at the meeting of the National Council of Teachers of English. New Orleans, Louisiana, 1974; O'Donnell, "Sexism in Language," *op. cit.*, pp. 1067-72; Rhome, "Manglish: What's It All About?" *op. cit.*; M.R. Schulz. "The Semantic Derogation of Women." B. Thorne and N. Henley, editors. *Language and Sex: Difference and Dominance.* Rowley, Massachusetts: Newbury House, 1975; R. Stanley. "Paradigmatic Women: The Prostitute." Paper presented at the meeting of the American Dialect Society. New York, N.Y., 1972; W.A. Sutton. "Sexual Fairness in Language." Ball State University, 1973. (Unpublished.); P. Tiedt and R. Semorile. "Semantic Discrepancies." *Elementary English* 50:1065-66; 1973. R. Todasco, E. Morgan, J. Sheridan, and K. Starr. *The Feminist English Dictionary.* Vol. I. Chicago: Loop Center YWCA, 1973.

[12]Sutton, "Sexual Fairness in Language," *op. cit.*, p. 10.

[13]Tiedt and Semorile, "Semantic Discrepancies," *op. cit.*, p. 1066.

3. *Subsuming terminology*. It is summarily assumed that, overall, masculine terms include or refer to females as well. Although sex-specific counterparts, such as craftsman/craftswoman, salesman/saleswoman, and governor/governess, are in frequent use, the complex lexical item assumes the masculine form, e.g., craftsmanship and salesmanship, presumably including female and male.[14] Since governess does not normally signify "one who governs" in the female form, the Honorable Ella Grasso is known as Connecticut's "governor." In addition, the counterparts patron/matron have evolved a third form for the female; since *matron* now refers to an older woman, the "helpful parenthood" of patron has evolved into *patroness* for the female disposed to helping a young artist.

4. *Woman as objects*. Many of the words and phrases used to describe women refer to food, flowers, and animals. Such terms as *angel*, *sugar*, and *cheesecake* are reserved for the female alone. Likewise, such phrases as *buttercup* and *sweet pea* are considered by some as complimentary terms for women; yet calling a man a pansy is tantamount to emasculating him. Words describing women tend to emphasize their bodies and physical attractiveness, while those referring to men characterize their intellectual or physical achievements or capabilities. Even in simplistic terms this bias is apparent — one speaks of Betty Grable's "great legs," and of Mickey Mantle's "great arm"; while one might also speak of Hirsch's "crazy legs," it surely is not meant in the same way as a reference to Grable.

The vocabulary patterns in English of naming, titles, and occupational language also merit closer scrutiny:

1. Naming is characterized by two distinct features: (a) the subsuming of identity by the female's traditional taking of the husband's name in marriage and the father's at birth, and (b) the representativeness of sex-expectations. Consistent with the traditional desire for a first-born male, many females are given names like Henrietta, Georgina, and Edwina. Less obvious, but equally emphatic, are those female names derived from male standards, e.g., Marla < Marlowe, Carla < Carl, Leslie < Lester, and Donna < Donald. The irony is that few could conceive of naming a male child after a female predecessor, with the exception of maiden names used as first or middle names. Even the maiden name, however, is masculine, for it was the surname of the woman's father. In addition, the meaning of first names in English reinforces the importance of the male, e.g., Val (strong), Roger (famous spear), Nicholas (victory), Robert (fame), and Martin (warlike). Yet names of women speak of more passive virtues: Gloria (worship), Mona (noble), and Judith (praised by the Lord).[15] In addition to the representative naming of children, Nilsen

---

[14]Nilsen and Nilsen, "Mr. and Mrs. Nilsen Debate Sexism in English," *op. cit., passim.*
[15]*Ibid.*

points out the representational naming of places, as the following mountain names illustrate: Nippletop (Adirondacks), Nipple Mountain, (Colorado), Nipple Peak (Texas), Nipple Butte (South Dakota), Squaw Peak (California), Maiden's Peak (Oregon), and Mary's Nipple (Utah). The source of naming in relation to topographical resemblance is obvious.

2. The patterning of titles in English affirms the subordinate role of women in a manner similar to that of naming. Marriage laws have, in essence, helped to institutionalize sexist language;[16] by giving the male the power to name the female, the law has served to perpetuate the status of male as master in a master-subject relationship. The title *Mrs.* conveys a total change of identity, while *Mr.* signifies a man, regardless of his marital status. The term *Mrs.* implies that "in and of themselves females are of no particular interest or importance and reflect[s] the assumption that marital status is *the* crucial fact of life for women."[17]

3. Occupational vocabulary of the language also attests to sexist bias. Such terms as authoress, poetess, female judge, and woman lawyer imply inequality between the sexes despite the fact that some women hold professional positions equal to those of men. According to Rhome, this pattern is derived from the assumption that "with the exception of occupations held by females [secretary, nurse, librarian, teacher, prostitute] most trades are generally accepted as male, unless the words 'woman,' 'female,' or the ending '-ess' is added."[18]

Although one might pursue a discussion of vocabulary and resulting images at greater length, the preceding illustrates the degree of prejudice against women in English vocabulary. Equally important, however, is sexist bias found in language structure.

The structure of a language encompasses the grammar, word formation patterns, and word choice and order that a speaker uses. The sexist bias in English structure can be illustrated most clearly by gender, suffixes, and generic patterns:

1. *Gender*. Although English pronouns are distinctly representative of gender, all nouns are claimed to be neuter. Gender is, therefore, linguistically determined by meaning; all nouns referring to living creatures are either feminine or masculine according to the sex of the individual, while all others remain neuter. Yet some nouns acquire attributive gender through rhetorical rather than grammatical use. The assumption that ships or storms are fe-

---

[16]J. Coryell. "What's In a Name?" *Women — A Journal of Liberation* 2: 59; 1972; H.S. Bosmajian. "The Language of Sexism." *ETC: A Review of General Semantics* 29: 305-13; 1972; Burr, Dunn, and Farquhar, *op. cit.*; Rhome, *op. cit.*

[17]Burr, Dunn, and Farquhar, "Women and the Language of Inequality," *op. cit.*, p. 843.

[18]Rhome, "Manglish: What's It All About?" *op. cit.*, p. 5.

male, for example, is derived from associative rather than structural characteristics.

2. *Suffixes*. The pattern of word formation which relies on suffixes to clarify meaning derives from the Latin patterns -ess/-er, -or which signify female and male. Although the structural linguists attempted to eradicate the pattern of forcing English grammar into Latin molds, these suffixes persist in diminutive and feminine forms, e.g., *suffragette, cigarette, heiress, laundress, sculptress, Jewess*. In essence, these suffixes imply that females are a special form of the "correct" male expression.

3. *Generic patterns*. Speakers of English have tended to subsume the female under the assumption that male terms stand for the entire population. Heavily documented evidence[19] attests to the fact that the most common pattern in English refers to the male as a hypothetical person: the man in the street, the man on the move, the land where our fathers died, our founding fathers, etc. The generic pattern allows men to stand for people in general and lets deeds of women and men be attributed to men alone. In cases where women are mentioned specifically, they are qualified as *pioneer women, peasant women*, and *beggar women*, erroneously implying that *pioneers, beggars*, and *peasants* are men. This exclusion of women in the male-oriented glossing of terms perpetuates the notion that people in general are men, and that woman is not one with the species of man, but a "distinct subspecies."[20]

The preceding illustrates, without question, male dominance in the English language. Lexically and structurally, English is so sexist that Rhome and Sutton have retermed it "Manglish." Although traditional linguists might regard the term just as absurd as the notion that random syllables, such as *a*men, *Her*cules, *man*date, *her*oin, and *boy*cott, have sexual significance, recent psycholinguistic studies have further reaffirmed the sexist bias by documentation of sex differences in language use.

## Sex Differences in Language Use

Although some studies[21] have found minimal or no formal differences between female and male language use, a number of other studies not only confirm the fact that there are, indeed, differences in the way women and men

---

[19]Burr, Dunn, and Farquhar, *op. cit.*; M.R. Key. "Linguistic Behavior of Male and Female." Linguistics 88: 15-31; 1972; Miller and Swift, *op. cit.*; E. Strainchamps. "Our Sexist Language." V. Gornick and B.K. Moran, editors. *Women in Sexist Society*. New York: Basic Books, Inc., Publishers, 1971. pp. 240-50; Sutton, *op. cit.*

[20]Miller and Swift, "One Small Step for Genkind," *op. cit.*, p. 36.

[21]S. Ervin-Tripp. "On Sociolinguistic Rules: Alternation and Co-occurrence." J.J. Gumperz and D. Hymes, editors. *The Ethnography of Communication*. New York: Holt, Rinehart and Winston, Inc., 1972. pp. 213-50.

speak, but also that these differences merit further investigation. In addition, the ethnocentric focus of most studies, which tend to center on white, middle- or upper-middle-class subjects, clearly indicates the need for additional research which pays attention to potential sexual differentiation in relation to race, ethnic origin, or socioeconomic class. Despite the need for more adequate research, the available literature, nonetheless, does substantiate differential use of language on the basis of sex.

Prior to 1960, most of the studies reported in the literature dealt with languages other than English. Frazer,[22] for example, documented the "special speech" used by Caffre women in South Africa. His evidence was derived primarily from the ascription of taboo words; those used by women fell into a category called Ukuteta Kwabafazi or "women's speech." Furley's[23] study documented sex contrasts in language usage common among tribes in Bengal, Bolivia, and the Lesser Antilles, and with Native Americans in the United States. He found differences not only in vocabulary, but in pronunciation and grammar as well. In addition, a study by Ekka[24] found a difference in verb paradigms in Kũrux depending on who speaks to whom, while Faust[25] found different pronoun series in Cocama.

Most recent studies that deal with English support Furley's findings, but the consensus appears to identify differences as characteristics of context and frequency rather than of exclusive language systems. Studies by Labov, Levine and Crockett, and Shuy, Wolfram, and Riley[26] documented evidence of the female's closer approximation to the norms of standard English; their findings also revealed that middle-class women exhibit more extreme patterns of hypercorrection than men. The differences, however, were attributed more to class than to sex. Trudgill's[27] study of urban British English supported the previously stated findings, but his interpretation gave the following reasons for the female's use of "correct" language forms:

1. Because of the subordinate position of women in America and England, it is more necessary for women to secure their social status linguistically.

[22]H.S. Frazer. *The Golden Bough*. London: Macmillan and Co., Ltd., 1900.

[23]P.H. Furley. "Men's and Women's Languages." *The American Catholic Sociological Review* 5: 218-23; 1955.

[24]F. Ekka. "Men's and Women's Speech in Kũrux." *Linguistics* 81: 25-31; 1972.

[25]N. Faust. "El lenguaje de los hombres y mujeres en Cocama." *Peru Indigena* 10: 115-17; 1953.

[26]W. Labov. *Social Stratification of English in New York City*. Washington, D.C.: Center for Applied Linguistics, 1966; L. Levine and H. Crockett. "Speech Variation in a Piedmont Community: Post-vocalic /r/." S. Lieberson, editor. *Explorations in Sociolinguistics*. The Hague: Mouton, 1966; R.W. Shuy, W.A. Wolfram, and W.K. Riley. *Linguistic Correlates of Social Stratification in Detroit Speech*. East Lansing, Michigan: Cooperative Research Project No. 6-1347, 1967.

[27]P. Trudgill. "Sex, Covert Prestige, and Linguistic Change in the Urban British English of Norwich." *Language in Society* 1: 179-95; 1972.

2. While men can be evaluated socially for what they do, women may be evaluated primarily on how they appear, physically and linguistically.

Additional studies report the male's more likely tendency to stutter[28] (attributed to America's emphasis on speech fluency of males over that of females); the likelihood of the speaker's sex being identified accurately by his/her speech patterns;[29] that men tend to talk more than women in mixed groups;[30] and that men interrupt women more than women interrupt men. This latter finding not only confirms male dominance but also refutes the popular belief that women are the "interrupters extraordinaire." Other studies[31] are less conclusive than the foregoing, which attests to the fact that the role of sex in communication has not yet been clearly defined.

The major conflict in classifying sex differences in language use, says Lakoff, stems from "the conflict not only between what women's speech is really like and what people think women's speech is really like, but also between what people think women's speech is like and what they think it should be like."[32] This conflict can be examined by considering vocabulary and structure, as well as such paralinguistic features as intonation and stress.

1. *Vocabulary*. The documentation of differences in women's vocabulary suggests that they stem mainly from four sources:[33] (a) women are barred from certain activities, a factor which consequently sex-types the vocabulary in a woman's domain; (b) women are not permitted the full range of taboo words and strong expletives considered acceptable for men; (c) women are re-

---

[28]R. Goldman. "Cultural Influences on the Sex Ratio in the Incidence of Stuttering." *American Anthropologist* 69: 78-81; 1967.

[29]C.C. Eble. "How the Speech of Some Is More Equal than Others." University of North Carolina, 1972. (Unpublished.)

[30]J. Kester. "In Other Words." *Chicago Sun Times*, May 7, 1972.

[31]R. Kibler, L. Barker, and D. Cegala. "Effect of Sex on Comprehension and Retention." *Speech Monographs* 37: 287-92; 1970; S.R. McCracken. "Comprehension for Immediate Recall of Time-compressed Speech as a Function of the Sex and Level of Activation of the Listener." *Speech Monographs* 36: 33; 1969; G. Goldhaber and C.H. Weaver. "Listener Comprehension of Compressed Speech When the Difficulty, Rate of Presentation, and Sex of the Listener Are Varied." *Speech Monographs* 35: 20-25; 1968; R.N. Bostrom and A.P. Kemp. "Type of Speech, Sex of Speaker, and Sex of Subject as Factors Influencing Persuasion." *Central States Speech Journal* 251-54; 1969.

[32]Lakoff, "Language and Woman's Place," *op. cit.*, p. 7.

[33]N. Barron. "Sex-Typed Language: The Production of Grammatical Case." *Acta Sociologica* 14: 24-42; 1971; D.W. Warshay. "Sex Differences in Language Style." C. Safilios-Rothschild, editor. *Toward a Sociology of Women*. Lexington, Massachusetts: Xerox, 1972. pp. 3-9; R.W. Shuy. "Sex as a Factor in Sociolinguistic Research." Paper presented at the meeting of the Anthropological Society of Washington. Washington, D.C., 1969; J. Hertzler. *A Sociology of Language*. New York: Random House, Inc., 1954; C. Kramer. "Women's Speech — Separate But Equal?" Paper presented at the meeting of the International Communications Association. Montreal, Quebec, 1973; P. Farb. *Word Play: What Happens When People Talk*. New York: Alfred A. Knopf, Inc., 1973; Lakoff, *op. cit.*; U. Weinrich. *Language in Contact*. The Hague: Mouton, 1964.

stricted from using vocabulary derived from task specializations related to sex; and (d) women are socialized to be submissive. These four sources seem to center around the fact that women and men represent different sex statuses for which varied value systems and behavioral orientations exist; language use, as cultural behavior, reflects these differences.

The use of adjectives by sex is perhaps the clearest illustration of vocabulary differences. In a number of both empirical and ethnographic studies,[34] women tended to use more adjectives that are frivolous or trivial, e.g., *cute*, *nice*, *lovely*, and they are more precise in their descriptions, evidenced by quantitative differences as well. Through a greater use of hyperbole,[35] qualifiers,[36] and nouns as objects rather than verbs as agents,[37] women's vocabulary, in short, mirrors their submissive role in society.

2. *Language structure*. The language of women tends to avoid strong statements and has connotations of uncertainty and triviality. Such phrases as *goodness* and *dear me* and the inherent politeness illustrated in the interrogative "Will you help me with this, please?" confirm this. In addition, women use questions quantitatively more than men,[38] use tag question formations more ("She's a charming woman, isn't she?")[39] and tend to leave sentences unfinished, e.g., "Well, I never . . ." These three structural features essentially indicate that women phrase their wishes in the form of requests, thereby avoiding a firm declaration which imposes the speaker's views on the listener. In asking a question, especially through the tag-formation, a woman can ask for confirmation of her idea; in being less decisive, one can always have an "out" and show that she is willing to be persuaded otherwise. Other studies document women's use of a creative style, while men's style is classified as empirical.[40] Another study found that females use significantly more words implying feeling, emotion, or motivation, more references to self, and more auxiliary and negative words, while males use significantly more words implying time, space, quantity, and destructive action.[41]

[34]Kramer, *op. cit.*; D.R. Entwistle and C. Garvey. *Adjective Usage*. Baltimore: Johns Hopkins University, Center for the Study of Social Organization of School, 1969; M. Farwell. "Women and Language." J.R. Leppaluto, editor. *Women on the Move*. Pittsburgh, Pennsylvania: KNOW, Inc., 1973. pp. 165-71; E. Toth. "How Can a Woman *Man* the Barricades? Or — Linguistic Sexism Up Against the Wall." *Women — A Journal of Liberation* 2: 57; 1970.

[35]O. Jespersen. *Language*. London: George Allen, Ltd., 1922.

[36]Lakoff, "Language and Woman's Place," *op. cit.*; P. Farb, *Word Play: What Happens When People Talk*, *op. cit.*

[37]Warshay, "Sex Differences in Language Styles," *op. cit.*; Barron, "Sex-Typed Language: The Production of Grammatical Case," *op. cit.*

[38]M.R. Key, "Linguistic Behavior of Male and Female," *op. cit.*

[39]Lakoff, "Language and Woman's Place," *op. cit.*

[40]Kramer, "Women's Speech — Separate But Equal?" *op. cit.*

[41]G.C. Gleser, L.A. Gottschalk, and J. Watkins. "The Relationship of Sex and Intelligence to Choice of Words: A Normative Study of Verbal Behavior." *Journal of Clinical Psychology* 15: 182-91; 1959.

3. *Paralanguage*. The paralinguistic features of women's language, such as intonation, pitch, and stress, tend to again confirm their subordinate role. While women are thought to have a greater intonational range than men, some intonation patterns, impressionistically the whining, questioning, "helpless" patterns are used predominately by women.[42] The higher pitch of females seems to represent the undesirable trait of timidness, while stress patterns are qualitatively submissive despite the patterns of hyperbole noted earlier. Lakoff even suggests that it is intonation rather than language structure which classifies women's speech as uncertain and subordinate.

Although some studies report conflicting results, a plethora of evidence suggests distinct differences in the speech of females and males. In order to resolve the conflict between "what women's speech is really like and what people think it should be like," we must take positive steps to erase sexist language.

## Alternatives and Solutions

Elimination of sexist bias in language, according to consensus of the literature cited here, focuses upon three alternatives:

1. We can change our consciousness and change our language as individuals;

2. We can legislate a few specific changes;

3. We can find the issue pointless and continue to use our old unconscious habit patterns of sexist speech reflecting the old sexist thinking.

The third alternative is simply out of the question, and the second is inherently absurd. Since one does not legislate respect, it would be ridiculous to say, for example, that "from this day forward we will not use feminine suffixes to represent occupations." Raising consciousness of both men and women and changing our individual language patterns, then, is the first and most plausible step for the elimination of sexist bias in language.

Considering the elements of this discussion, I propose four alternatives to end sexism in the English language:

1. *Dictionary*. Female and male gender words should be equally represented in illustrative sentences and used in a wide variety of contexts. Stereotyped roles should be avoided when gender words are used, and the use of the generic "man" when referring to humanity should be excluded.

2. *Vocabulary*. As women and men, we must broaden our vocabularies to include words that are known to us but that are socially sex typed. In essence,

[42]Kramer, "Women's Speech — Separate But Equal?" *op. cit.*; Eble, "How the Speech of Some Is More Equal Than Others," *op. cit.*; Lakoff, "Language and Woman's Place," *op. cit.*

we must begin to use words that say exactly what we mean. Is that not, after all, the purpose of language?

3. *Generics and suffixes.* As alternatives to the generic *he*, we can substitute nouns for nominative pronouns, possessive nouns for possessive pronouns, and appropriate plural pronouns for inappropriate male-only singular pronouns. Inappropriate suffixes and qualifiers should be eliminated.

4. *Sex differences in language use.* Most of the studies cited in this discussion confirm the fact that there are systems of co-occurring, sex-linked linguistic signals in American English. If we are to eliminate sexism in language, we must continue to conduct thorough, linguistically sound research to determine actual sex-differences and seriously question the validity of their perpetuation. As Shuy noted, "We have been so busy trying to understand what is said that we pay little conscious attention to how it is said."[43] In truth, how something is said frequently says more than the actual words.

The male dominance and sex-typing of English and its use have been documented extensively over the past decade. It is time to heed the researchers and consciously begin to eliminate sexist bias in language, not only in schools where most of the attention is now, but in our other socializing institutions as well. As women increase their independence in life styles and choices, so, too, men are becoming more liberated from traditional patriarchal roles. For language, this "human liberation" means that we must be able to *humanly* express our feelings, beliefs, knowledge, aspirations, and values through a medium of expression suited to our needs. If the primary function of language is to interpret and express the form and content of our lives, we must revise, extend, and refine the language system we use to accommodate our increasingly more varied strata of human experience.

[43]R.W. Shuy, "Sex as a Factor in Sociolinguistic Research," *op. cit.*, p. 3.

# 9

# Multiculturalism in the U.S.A. Has Worldwide Implications

Florence Makita Yoshiwara

*We are all citizens of one world, we are all of one blood. To hate man because he was born in another country, because he speaks a different language, or because he takes a different view on this subject or that, is great folly. Desist, I implore you, for we are all equally human. . . .Let us have but one end in view, the welfare of humanity.*

— *John Amos Comenius (1592-1670)*

Is what we have proclaimed as multicultural education compatible with Comenius's statement? Should multicultural education also be practiced with the broader sense of understanding and accepting cultures throughout the world? And how important are such questions in our continuing struggle for multicultural education in the United States? Let us first look at the view of multicultural education and its implications for our society from the context of our changing society and world.

Have we stopped to consider the student and his/her view of our society and what implications that has for education as a whole? There is no question about what we face in our everyday world, a nation molded by an exploding techno-industrial society. Demands created by industry and consumers have created the greatest diversity in goods and services known to humankind. This diversity has created a supermarket of goods — clothes, cars, etc. — a veritable overabundance of choices in our everyday life. This is the real experience of every student in our schools.

We need to acknowledge that this diversity has accelerated a destandardization of life styles in the United States. Part of the evidence we see in our schools is the variety in modes of dress which have become an accepted pattern — long dresses, short dresses, long hair, short hair, jeans, tennis shoes, and platform heels have all become part of the accepted style. Panicky parents have blamed the permissive society, not realizing that the roots of this diversity lie in our techno-industrial society, of which they themselves are the demanding clients.

Despite these obvious changes in our society, education has continued to balk at facilitating real changes in our schools. Most schools are still rooted in the concepts of an earlier industrial society — with regimentation the order of the day, and the puritan ethic the pervasive ideal in the curriculum — with no suggestion of alternatives. We are still persisting in ill-preparing our students for the real world of change and diversity.

"While industry is highly responsive to consumer demand, the student consumer is forced to fight to make the education industry responsive to his/her demand for diversity."[1] Herein lies the basic contradiction in the world of the student.

Multicultural education is an important tool for implementing the kinds of changes in curriculum which reflect the reality of life in a culturally pluralistic society and world. It verifies the students' real world from the sense of both the majority and the minority student. It both reflects diversity and suggests alternatives that are part of reality.

Never before have we had the opportunity to learn so much about the world we inhabit — its people, its natural resources, its technological potential. What then are the issues as they relate to multiculturalism in the United States and its implications for understanding and accepting cultures throughout the world?

The issues are threefold: (a) the necessity of studying root cultures to give dignity to and create acceptance of nonwhite minorities; (b) the necessity of studying root cultures as a means of learning about alternatives and change; and (c) the relationships created by the expanding interdependence of world nations.

In the area of the study of root cultures there still remains a great deal of confusion. Teachers are still using the study of foreign cultures to fulfill mandates to include multicultural education in their curriculum. This does very little to recognize that nonwhite minorities in this country possess a culture which is an amalgamation of both their root culture and their experience here. There is a dramatic difference in the two experiences.

[1] Alvin Toffler. *Future Shock*. New York: Random House, Inc., 1970. p. 272.

The past experience of minority peoples here has been one of economic oppression and a dehumanizing process coupled with tyranny as a "justification." Their root cultures have often been considered a "hindrance" to their
assimilation. Non-English speaking students are viewed as "disadvantaged."
In order to achieve dignity, students need to develop a respect for the root
culture as well as to recognize the uniqueness of the experience in this
country. The two are inseparable parts of the whole nonwhite minority
person.

Students are all ingrained with the greatness of ancient Rome and Greece
as part of their social studies programs. Yet they have been acclimated to accept omission of the study of the highly developed cultures of Africa, Asia,
and the Americas as a matter of little consequence. Of greater damage to
nonwhite students has been the study of their root culture as strange, primitive, or exotic, with little attempt made to explore their common bonds of
humanity.

An example would be the Asian cultures which are in reality (Asians being
60 percent of the world population) a majority culture in this world. The
ancient culture of China goes back further as a continuous culture than do
those of Greece and Rome, and furthermore has maintained a written language which is still used today with little modification.

"Now the *I Ching,* a major book in the countercultures which has all the
young tossing coins or yarrow stalks, is the oldest book on the planet. It goes
back to about 2000 B.C. It is the basic structure of information and a model-
ing of consciousness and time, and is, if you read Carl Jung's introduction to
it, rather a sophisticated document and not just a piece of oracle supersti-
tion."[2]

Alex Haley's miraculous discovery of his African roots presents another
dimension to the validity of studying root cultures. He states, " . . . we black
people — probably more than any other people on the face of earth in as
large a number — have the most common generic background: that every
single one of us without exception ancestrally goes back to some one of those
[African] villages, belongs to some one of those tribes, was captured in some
way, was put on some one of those slave ships, sailed across the same ocean
into some succession of plantations . . . ."[3] His story of his experience ex-
plores the relationship of black Americans to Africa — not just the historical,
but also the emotional ties which are real today.

Without the study of root cultures there is little understanding of the experience of nonwhite peoples in the United States. Granted they became

---

[2]William Irwin Thompson. "Lindisfarne: Education for a Planetary Culture." Robert R.
Leeper, editor. *Emerging Moral Dimensions in Society: Implications for Schooling.* Washington, D.C.: Association for Supervision and Curriculum Development, 1975. p. 66.

[3]Alex Haley. "In Search Of." *The Oral History Review.* 1973.

victimized in our racist society, but there is such a difference in their interaction with the majority society. And the manner in which each group dealt
with racism has been little understood except in stereotypic jargon.

The wild, wild West, as an example, would never have been so without the
stubborn resistance of the proud Native Americans defending long established cultures and life styles. Certainly they existed long before the coming
of the white man. Would it not add to the understanding of the wild, wild
West to explore the cultures and life styles of the Native Americans?

## A Nation of Immigrants

What is being suggested is that no cultures, for example, ancient Greece
and Rome, should be studied as the only pattern upon which our country was
developed. We are, after all, a nation of immigrants; therefore the influences
of all world cultures do exist. Nonwhite students need this kind of reenforce-
ment of their heritage, and white students need to understand the many influences which have always been an important part of our culture.

While education has, in the past, been recognized as a tool for the formation of character, it has also meant the channeling of youth into traditional
value systems which have lost relevance to our present diverse and changing
society. In response, educators have been thrown into a frenzied search for
changes in curriculum which might reflect movement into the future.

Unfortunately many of these changes have been technical adaptations of
methods to continue the instilling of old data. Computer-assisted education,
television, audio visuals, programmed instruction, and PPBS are but a few
examples of these new techniques. Many of these "changes" have also been
adopted in the name of better return on the tax dollar.

Multicultural education, through the study of root cultures of nonwhite
peoples, can be an important tool for preparing students for technological or
social change. The basic premise of multicultural education is "I'm okay,
you're okay, and furthermore, your ways are okay and so are mine." In this
new learned ability to accept diversity, a student develops the ability to look
at his/her world and the world of others in a more objective manner. Since
differences can be positive, change and alternatives are no longer a threaten-
ing issue.

Thus freed, we can look at other cultures and accept from them solutions
to problems which we could not find in our own, or a fresh approach to problem solving found in "other" life styles. Because of what our techno-industrial society is rapidly doing to our environment, we are beginning to appreciate the respect for nature which has long been the central concern of Asians
and Native Americans.

"Sometimes, as we work toward a multicultural curriculum, a concept borrowed from another, and older culture can bring new insight. So it is with the concept of 'living use,' borrowed from Zen."[4] Living use speaks about the concern for the preservation of the environment which is highly relevant to our present day problems. Some of the examples Mitsuo Adachi uses are: "There is no living use of the electricity when the room is vacant; a textbook closed and in the desk has no living use; and water running while you are brushing your teeth has no living use."[5] Here is a thought dealing with ecology which had its origins 2500 years ago.

Cultural anthropology has demonstrated that there are numerous other examples which illustrate the study of root cultures as an effective manner of discovering old solutions to our present-day crises. These alternatives exist particularly in the root cultures of nonwhite peoples in this country.

The issue of the interdependence of nations is one about which most of us are aware. The daily newspapers, television, and radio remind us of our involvements throughout the world whether it be Arabian oil, detente with Russia, Vietnamese refugees, apartheid in Africa, relations with China, or the Lockheed scandal. How does this relate to multicultural education?

As nonwhite peoples in the United States, we are keenly aware of how international issues still affect how we as Asian Americans are perceived. At the Japanese American Citizens League Convention in Washington, D.C., a few years ago, while we were waiting to have our portrait taken in front of the Capitol building, a group of demonstrators came marching by in protest of the purchasing of foreign goods to the detriment of domestic industry. Some in the group began to hurl epithets at us Japanese Americans, accusing us of being responsible for this problem, when in reality they were referring to trade with Japan.

This was another harsh reminder of the fact that of all nonwhite peoples, Asian Americans are still perceived as foreign, even though they may have been in this country for four and five generations. They are still consistently asked, even hesitatingly by the most "informed" people, "Where were you born?" or "Do you speak Chinese?" and if not, why not. Such persistent attitudes serve as a constant reminder that Asian Americans still need to be acutely aware of foreign relations, because of the impact it has upon our acceptance or nonacceptance as Americans. What is American and what is foreign needs to be clearly defined in curriculum, reading materials, texts, films, and classroom activities in order to overcome the stereotyping and the resultant injustices inflicted upon nonwhite students, especially Asian Americans.

This was the issue which, in the minds of the uninformed public, "legiti-

---

[4]Mitsuo Adachi. "Living Use: Example of a Multicultural Approach." *Educational Leadership* 33 (3): 189; December 1975.

[5]*Ibid.*

mized" the concentration camp experience of 110,000 persons of Japanese ancestry in this country during World War II. It is important to note that two-thirds of these persons were American citizens by birth. Many leaders of the Asian American community and other nonwhite communities are uncertain that such an act might not be repeated in the hysteria of a comparable crisis involving another nonwhite nation.

"Today, more people throughout the world are trying to understand each other, but a willingness is not enough. It takes careful attention and concern."[6] In spite of the technological advances which have brought us physically closer together, education must be concerned that the separation in the minds of people, that crucial gap, has hardly begun to be closed. This schism will have disastrous results in our present era of the interdependence of nations.

Multicultural education is after all a basic undertaking through which we call for the recognition of the common humanity of all people, not only in the culturally pluralistic nation in which we live, but also in the culturally pluralistic world. The time is NOW. If we ignore this reality we may all be in great jeopardy.

[6]Seymour Fersh, editor. *Learning About Peoples and Cultures.* Evanston, Illinois: McDougal, Littell & Co., 1974.

# 10

# Cultural Pluralism and Culturism: The International Dimension

Allen A. Schmieder and Mary F. Crum

## A Two-Way Street

The quality of American life is being increasingly enriched by the nation's growing awareness and support of cultural diversity; yet, in spite of this fact, much of what we continue to teach our young children about the rest of the world is racist, ignorant, and contradictory to this significant national movement.[2] While this new direction in American education and society toward a recognition of the advantages and potential power of cultural pluralism may be the most important happening in this nation in this century, *a strong international perspective would add much to what we need to know and understand about our own internal cultural character, and our own diverse cultural character provides an ideal vehicle for improving our knowledge and understanding of the rest of the world.*

Yet a cursory analysis of many of the most recent and popular materials on multicultural education shows that little attention is being given to making these international linkages. As we develop new curricula that are more sen-

The opinions expressed in this chapter are the personal views of the authors and do not necessarily reflect the positions or views of the U.S. Office of Education or the National Council for the Social Studies.

[1] A neologism introduced by the authors to imply a cultural-level prejudice analogous to racism. A doctrine that inherent differences among the various world cultures determine the relevant achievement or "progress" of those cultures, usually involving the idea that one's own culture is superior to others.

[2] Similar statements could be made for other nations of the world — and an example is given on pp. 82-83 — but this chapter, following the general theme of the book, focuses on the situation in the United States.

sitive to the many culture worlds that exist within American society, there is an increasing need to build them within an international context that not only relates accurately to roots and relationships where they exist, but one that also provides a framework for a new global ethic regarding cultural pluralism — an ethic that espouses the virtues of cultural diversity and respects the integrity and strengths of all individual cultures.

This chapter is in no way an attempt to present accurately the googol-plexity of the world's cultures — or even symbolically represent the excitement of its inestimable variety. That delightful explanation and exploration is left to the scholars of the social studies and its member disciplines — and many have already contributed substantially toward that end. What follows is intended only to call attention to what seems to be an inequity in the growing national dialogue about cultural pluralism and hopefully to stimulate some thoughtful consideration of how educators might expand our internal objectives in this important area to include a determination to reduce some long-standing shortcomings in the way we evaluate cultures worldwide.

## Some Examples of Culturism

Following are some brief examples of the kind of culturism we are concerned about:

• Many American children learn that Christopher Columbus "proved" the earth to be round in 1492 — when Eratosthenes, a Greek scholar working in Egypt in the third century B.C., not only knew that the earth was round, but calculated its circumference with considerable accuracy. Whether or not American children learn that Columbus or someone else proved the earth to be round is not nearly as important as the fact that few American children learn of the exciting discoveries of Eratosthenes and others who worked and studied in the libraries of Babylonia, Alexandria, and other centers of culture in the pre-Christian Islamic world.

• U.S. students learn that the world's "first" oil well, Drake's Well, was drilled in Titusville, Pennsylvania — several years after a number of wells had been successfully completed in Eastern Europe.

• Certain history texts emphasize how the Phoenicians, residents of one of the "cradles of Western civilization," were the first to venture onto the high seas — although Indians living along the Asian sub-continent's Malabar coast, a part of one of the "cradles of Eastern civilization," not only were plying the ocean many years before the Phoenicians, but were operating on a far more vast and treacherous body of water.

• Moveable block printing appeared in the West some six centuries after it was known in China and the first type printing in Europe began around 1450, approximately 400 years after the Chinese invention. Yet when talking about the mainsprings of the printing world, we generally give the best copy to Gutenberg and his famous press and rarely mention the Asiatic foundations of this very important process.

• Sports fanatics who have come to consider fall weekends and football to be synonymous feel that there is nothing that is more of the American culture than football. Yet there is some evidence that people were kicking a ball around prior to the days of recorded history. There is documentation that the ancient Greeks played the foot-kicking ball game of *harpaston,* and variations of "football" were played in 12th century England.

These are but a few examples of the kind of "dominant culture view" that exists in many educational programs. Cases relating to some popular mythologies and games were selected to exaggerate the message. Whether or not they are good examples is unimportant. There is an almost unlimited supply of examples of culturism — covering the full spectrum of education and society — that could be identified to support the case. But the purpose here is not to call for an exhaustive list of the culturist views of Americans or to demand that all such biased elements be purged from educational programs, but to ask that educators develop ways to educate children about this or any other nation in such a way as to give them great pride and love for their native land, while at the same time creating a high level of respect and appreciation for other places and cultures.

The "center of the universe" approach used by the Monarch in *The King and I,* is probably not the best way to accomplish this dual objective. And the "chamber of commerce" approach used in many classrooms and curricula in the United States is not much different from the orientation of that erstwhile King of Siam. It must be noted here that there has been some decline in this "first is best" approach over the last several years. A few social scientists have even become alarmed that we have downgraded the importance of competition so much in the pursuit of cooperation, touching, and feeling, that sometime in the future education will be faced with the crisis of trying to find ways to get children to compete and be motivated toward excellence.

## Some General Causes of the Problem

There is a great paradox that exists in American education and society that makes the problem of achieving a more culturally balanced view of the world even more difficult than it might otherwise be: Americans profess global leadership, want the rest of the world to examine closely our culture and the successes of our national experiment — many even feel that other countries would be better off if they pursued the "American way of life." Yet, as a people, we probably know less about the world we strive to proselytize than do our educated counterparts in much of the rest of the world. We are relatively ignorant of the basic geographic, historic, and economic characteristics of other nations and regions — especially those which are considered to be members of the "Third World." Again, a few examples to make the point:

• The Middle East is of crucial importance to current United States and world affairs — and news of what is going on in the region has become a daily event in the national media — yet the average American could not accurately delineate the extent of the Middle East, let alone describe its basic natural, historical, and cultural character, or its most crucial developmental problems.

• "Detente" and relationships with communist nations have been at the center of the political and military thinking of this nation for over four decades; yet most Americans cannot even identify the majority of the 15 communist states in the world, let alone intelligently analyze their internal nature or culture. Even educated Americans know little of the cultural diversity of the U.S.S.R. or of the impact of that diversity upon the development of that important nation.

• Many talk about "Africans" as if they are of one kind and culture no matter where they live in the trans-Sahara part of that vast, second largest of the world's continents. Emphasis is given to the jungle (there is very little); jungle animals (most live in the grasslands); Bushmen, Pygmies, and Watusi (approximately one-half of one percent of the sub-Saharan population); people living in primitive villages headed by despotic chiefs (most primitive villages are gone and almost every conceivable political system has been tried). Although we proudly talk of the diversity of American culture (and rightly so), a strong case could be built to show that there is even greater diversity of culture in Africa.

And the beat goes on. It does not take much high-powered reasoning to conclude that such minimal knowledge about other cultures is sure to result in maximum misunderstanding toward those cultures. One thing that psychologists and sociologists generally agree upon is that it is difficult for people to develop empathy for people and places with which they are unfamiliar.

## Varying Degrees of Knowledge and Culturism

When speaking so cavalierly regarding the knowledge of millions of persons about the rest of the world, it is important to reemphasize a position presented earlier in this chapter: the authors mean only to highlight some apparently widespread culturist views and causes. We do not believe that everyone in this country is equally ill-informed or that educators are not making considerable progress on many fronts in improving our understanding of other nations. Americans do not all look at other cultures in the same way, nor do they have equal information about them. There are obviously great differences and these are influenced by many things including ethnic background, location and character of places lived, education, and work experience. Americans with strong roots in a particular foreign culture, for example, would obviously see that culture in a quite different way than would citizens with ties to some other part of the world. Americans whose business or profession relates to other cultures are sometimes among the most culturally cosmopolitan people in the world. (It can also be said, unfortunately, that many Americans whose work takes them into other nations show little interest in learning anything about the culture visited.)

It should also be emphasized that much of the apathy which many Americans have had toward the rest of the world stems from the strong political and economic independence and high level of internal stability that have characterized this nation throughout most of its history. But with increasing international interdependence it will become necessary to know more and more about other regions and cultures if we are to understand them fully, and interact positively with them.

## Culturism Is a Worldwide Phenomenon

It is important to accentuate the fact that Americans do not have a corner on ignorance toward other places and cultures. All nations of the world are to some degree ethnocentric and culturist — many much more so than the United States. Because this treatise is concerned with the extent of these conditions in the United States, an example of foreign culturism is presented only to provide some needed perspective. The example to demonstrate this point is presented at some risk for it touches upon what many believe to be the most potentially powerful political movement of this century (if we are going to set about developing a new international ethic, we might as well bore right in!) — the controversial call for a "New International Economic Order." First introduced at the United Nations Conference on Man and the Biosphere, the phrase has since become a popular slogan of both the "Third World" and the Communist Bloc — comprising approximately one-half of the world's nations. The majority of the proponents of this new economic order feel that much of the affluence of the United States and other countries in the Western world has come at the expense of the Third World. The following statement from a paper prepared for the Belgrade International Workshop on Environmental Education aptly characterizes the position:

. . . It is vital, therefore, to take measures that will prevent a certain type of economic growth and anarchical industrialization from having harmful repercussions on the great mass of the population. . . . The growing and, at times, unrestrained consumption pressure by certain sections of humanity with regard to the earth's resources, their irrational exploitation and the establishment of inequitable norms in their international marketing, lead gradually to an irreversible crisis and bar the possibility of a just life to millions of human beings. . . . There must, therefore, be a radical change that will make it possible to achieve new styles of development, whose goal will be the proper utilization and equitable distribution of each country's resources . . . also involves a change in the order of priorities established generally by a few groups at the world level. In this connection those policies aimed at the exclusive maximization of output, without regard for its consequences on society and on the resources available for improving the quality of human life, must be opposed.[3]

Because there has been some exploitation, because the world's media — and sometimes governments — tend to emphasize negative experiences, and because of increasing internal and external political militancy on the part of Third World countries, such a viewpoint is understandable. But in the opinion of the authors, it is a culturist measure of things and reflects considerable ignorance about the development of Western nations and cultures. For example, the United States, which has traditionally had the highest per capita consumption rate in the world, has been relatively self-sufficient throughout its modern history. Year in and year out, over 90 percent of the U.S. gross national product has been produced and consumed within the boundaries of the nation. And the productive capacity which has been generated in connection with this country's phenomenal economic growth has resulted in a resource-building capability that has been used to facilitate healthy and needed development in many regions and cultures of the world. (That there have not been greater efforts toward international cooperation in resource and economic development is unfortunate — but it is not a point to be explored here.)

Given the current world atmosphere, it is important to work for the clearest possible understanding not only of the nature of the cultures of other nations but of the political and economic forces that are an inseparable part of those cultures. There has been, and there will continue to be, abuses and misunderstandings — as is usually the case when markedly different cultures interact — but improvement in trans-national communication and education should rapidly diminish such potentially volatile viewpoints.

It has become the hackneyed slogan of nearly every new educational movement in recent history — and that in itself should tell us something important about the relationship between rapid change and educational renewal — but

[3]Position statement of certain Third World nations drafted for consideration by the UNEP-UNESCO sponsored International Workshop on Environmental Education. Belgrade, Yugoslavia, October 13-22, 1975.

it must be said that *meaningful multicultural educational reform will require new approaches on the part of the entire educational community.* But most of all, there is need for a reaffirmation of the central importance of the social studies in the American educational system. Since Sputnik, education decision makers have generally given the social studies the lowest priority among the "basic" subjects. For over a decade now educators have said that it is most important that young children learn to compute (work their mathematics) and communicate (read). Educational budgets have generally reflected this bias and the media have relentlessly emphasized the indispensability of both subjects. These skills are essential to live and prosper in this or any other nation or culture, but they are of secondary importance to the development of a good understanding and respect for all peoples and cultures and a strong commitment to raising the quality of life of all humankind.

## Some Recommendations for Reducing Culturism

The following are recommended as positive actions toward improving international understanding and reducing culturism. Because of space limitations, the recommendations are brief and serve only as introductions to some needs and possible program alternatives.

• *The need for program development guidelines — both at the national and international levels.* Although many educators have experience in the area of multicultural education and there is a growing body of literature on the subject, there is a healthy diversity of opinion about the nature and meaning of the concept. Some basic guidelines need to be drawn from the best thinking, experience, and research that have taken place to date. Two examples of recent efforts at such a synthesis are the *Curriculum Guidelines for Multiethnic Education*[4] developed by the National Council for the Social Studies and *A Guide for Improving Public School Practices in Human Rights*[5] prepared by the Phi Delta Kappa Teacher Education Project on Human Rights. It is hoped that international education organizations and associations will develop similar positive statements.

• *A search for the common ground.* It is generally believed that cultural variety is a healthy condition for any nation and that the excitement of living in the world will always be somewhat proportional to the differences that exist from place to place. If such a view is true then everything possible should be done to strengthen and preserve diversity in the human way of life.

---

[4]*Curriculum Guidelines for Multiethnic Education.* Position statement of the National Council for the Social Studies, 1976.

[5]Phi Delta Kappa Teacher Education Project on Human Rights. *A Guide for Improving Public School Practices in Human Rights.* Bloomington, Indiana: Phi Delta Kappa, 1975.

But there are some cultural characteristics that are "global," for example, the importance of human dignity, and these should be articulated and used as a basis for improved communication and understanding across the world. An exploration of these shared values will not only identify some of the sinews of future international cooperation but the search should also help to emphasize the great extent of the differences that exist from place to place.

• *The real experts.* Although there are many good reasons that the basic materials for any course of study that focuses on foreign cultures should be developed by Americans, there is no good reason that there should not be increased input by educators from the nations and cultures under study. Participation could take place in many forms ranging from substantive reviews to authorship. In addition, it might be advisable for U.S. educators, who are using more and more original manuscripts and documents in their courses, to incorporate similar materials from the cultures under study.

• *A new kind of gatekeeper.* There is a corps of sophisticated, well-trained "experts" who have been admirably holding down the international education front during the past several decades of worldwide change and tension. They have worn many hats and have related in many different ways to a myriad of organizations, causes, and political pressures. And they have juggled magnificently. With the increased mobility of educators of all kinds and the exploding growth in worldwide connectedness in recent years, it is probable that it will never again be possible for a small group of international specialists to fully represent us on all fronts. It seems logical then that ways should be devised for this well-trained cadre to switch its focus from one of essentially doing the job alone, to one of managing and coordinating the thousands of relatively inexperienced educators who will be moving in and out of the international arena in the future.

• *From a flirtation to a beginning.* Over the past decade, increasing numbers of Americans have become involved in what have popularly been called "countercultures." People of all ages have taken up yoga, learned about Zen, and tried to read Chinese fortune stones. Transcendental meditation has become a popular college course. Numerous other examples could be given. These experiences provide invigorating infusions from other cultures and have the potential to open up whole new vistas to the persons involved. But such practices are essentially no more than flirtations with other worlds and often lead to even further misunderstanding about other cultures. In addition, many educational programs symbolize foreign cultures with peripheral frills; with ancient relics, museum oddities, and exotic dances. There is nothing wrong with introducing some of the more picturesque and esoteric customs of a culture, but they should not be presented as the core of what it is that another people is all about. There needs to be a greater effort to expose students more fully and realistically by helping them to understand other cultural values — what it is that makes others "tick."[6]

• *Toward changes in attitudes and behaviors — more than improving cognition or adding information.* Despite the sensitivity generally aroused by any suggestions of influencing or changing anyone's behavior, it is more important than ever that attempts be made to do so in the area of cultural interaction. Much of the public furore about declining achievement in the social studies (as well as in several other subjects) has been a reaction to lowering scores on tests which essentially measure factual knowledge. The way we feel and act toward other peoples and cultures is far more important than knowing a few basic facts about them. An objective examination cannot measure one's feeling about the beauty of Indian jewelry or the taste of curry.

• *Need for a more thorough analysis of these and other alternative approaches to improving cultural pluralism.* Because most educators have only recently become concerned about formally and systematically advocating cultural pluralism, there are advances on many fronts — but some are necessarily moving without a lot of information regarding cause and effect. It is possible that some well-intended efforts to preserve cultural diversity could in fact be destroying it. Some experts, for example, feel that the quickest way to weaken minority cultures and move even faster toward homogeneity is to mount highly publicized and well-financed programs directed as "strengthening" minority cultures.

In such programs, to cite but two possibilities, the financing and activities are usually determined by the dominant culture and are therefore likely to be biased against the groups supposedly being served; and the new programs may increase the interaction between cultures and result in considerable blending where cultures overlap. It would obviously be impossible for all of the world's cultures to live in isolation in order to protect forever their separate heritage and customs. Even so, there must be some ways of coexistence and sharing that will be better than others. Recent history is filled with poor and sometimes even tragic examples of intercultural relationships. It is time to develop an equally impressive array of examples of how such relationships really should be formed and managed.

## Now. Tomorrow at the Latest

The rapid rate of progress and improvement that has occurred in this highly critical sector of the curriculum over the past decade of American education gives considerable confidence — not only in the fact that the education

[6]Carlos E. Cortés. "Concepts and Strategies for Multiethnic Education." *Social Science Education Consortium Newsletter.* November 1975, pp. 3-4.

of our children is in good hands, but in the care of those who are unusually sensitive to what is happening in the world. But the situation is becoming so dynamic that there is no room for satisfaction or self-congratulation. The world is growing, blossoming, exploding, in ways that exceed any past experience. There is a great need to reconsider even the best and most flexible of our educational approaches and curriculums — to find new ways to modernize and continually renew our interactions with and interpretations of other peoples and nations. Now. Tomorrow at the latest. It is not only a matter of more effectively responding to the continuing revolution and accelerating change that much of society is now caught up in, but of overcoming the years of negligence that resulted from our necessary focus on internal matters. We have tried to understand our own culture and have tended to be introspective — it is now time to draw closer to other cultures and in the process perhaps better understand ourselves.

# 11

# Where Peoples Meet: Thoughts on Research in Multicultural Education

Kaoru Yamamoto

In multicultural education, as in few other realms of our endeavor, research is severely taken to task for its functions as well as for its modes of operation. It is here, where different peoples meet, that most of our allegedly objective explorations of human affairs are shown to be inescapably subjective in nature. It is here, where varied cultures interact, that much of our ostensibly vast understanding of human dynamics proves to be unmistakably narrow and shallow in character.

In an uncelebrated article on research in education a decade ago,[1] I summarized the views of many astute observers of science in order to call attention to the fact that most of us lack the special sort of intimacy with life that is indispensable to the asking of significant questions and to a full appreciation of human complexities. Sheer acquaintance with the phenomenon under study is not enough, and inert knowledge as a passerby is insufficient, since this so-called "phenomenon under study" unavoidably involves *us*. The stream of life does not merely flow by us; it immerses us all in interaction. Thus, our act of exploration is itself a part and parcel of the explored scene.

These observations probably need to be repeated in relation to our deliberation on research in multicultural education. This is partly because the field cannot afford traditional technician-experts in the divisive sociobehavioral disciplines, who tend to isolate and denigrate the main character, the per-

[1] Kaoru Yamamoto. "A Reflection upon Research in Education." *Journal of Teacher Education* 19: 486-94; Winter 1968.

son.[2] It is also because multicultural education is itself an effort to develop in its participants a deeper level of intimacy with what *Homo sapiens* is about, with its roots, development, potential, and glory and folly. Needless to say, if multicultural education meant nothing but a cafeteria presentation of specific information on separate subgroups of earthlings, it would add little to the idea of all in one and one in all, or the important sense of the interrelatedness of human fate.

## A Partnership

"Nature may be neutral," said Lynd in his 1939 classic, *Knowledge for What?* "But culture is not neutral, because culture is interested personalities in action."[3] These individuals in action and interaction are not inanimate objects merely reactive to the intervention of someone or something else, but active beings who strive, under any circumstances, to structure and restructure their life space in pursuit of their existential meaning.[4] In fact, the myriad ways of this structuring and restructuring process are what is represented in the concept of culture. These efforts are through the diverse means of technological development and economic deployment of material resources, creation and uses of symbol systems (language, arts, beliefs-values, rituals, etc.), and generation and maintenance of social institutions (familial, schooling, healing, religious, commercial, warfare, political, legal, etc.).

As a purposive being with dignity and integrity, a person's involvement in any research attempts ought to be as a full partner, and not as a subject, respondent, or informant under someone else's unilateral control. From the planning phase through the completion of a project, the so-called "natives" should be equal status collaborators, and something of value must remain with the cooperating culture. Obviously this requires quite a bit of reorientation in the traditional researchers who are used to the posture of knowing, external authority engaged in an exploitative project. The needed rethinking is epitomized in two thumbnail sketches, paraphrased below from the descriptions given by a Filipino scholar.[5]

Some researchers are the so-called *data exporters,* that is, those who conduct their studies safari style, taking away everything they can by way of data

[2] Kenneth Boulding. "Comment on 'The Unity of Social Sciences'." *Human Organization* 34: 332; Winter 1975; Muzafer Sherif. "If the Social Scientist Is to be More Than a Mere Technician . . . ." *Journal of Social Issues* 24: 41-61; January 1968.

[3] Robert S. Lynd. *Knowledge for What?: The Place of Social Science in American Culture.* New York: Grove Press, Inc., 1964. p. 182.

[4] Viktor E. Frankl. *The Will to Meaning.* New York: The New American Library, Inc., 1969.

[5] G. Tagumpay-Castillo. As quoted in: Richard W. Brislin, Stephen Bochner, and Walter J. Lonner, editors. *Cross-Cultural Perspectives on Learning.* New York: Sage Publications, Inc., 1975. p. 9.

and leaving nothing of value to the host culture. These are also called the *hit-and-run* types. In contrast, there are *idea stimulators* who help raise pertinent questions and formulate suitable plans of inquiry so that the hosting people themselves may find meaningful answers and workable solutions through projects of their own. Since these *facilitators* are competent and secure, they do not require any ego trips at the expense of their collaborators. Obviously, what research in multicultural education needs is a corps of facilitators, not one of safari hunters.

The desired catalytic function may well be performed by the action research approach. Here, to answer questions of practical significance, everyday experience is studied by first introducing a change in it and then observing the results. This Lewinian model consists of a spiral of cycles of the problem identification and analysis, fact-finding, conceptualization, action planning, execution, and evaluation of the results.[6] In this process, the experts are not the typical, segregated investigators known for their "non-participant, non-rescue reaction."[7] Instead, they are supportive comrades of the teachers, students, parents, and administrators in cooperative efforts to explore, understand, and improve the latter's endeavors. Basically, the question is the practitioners', and, most of all, the whole experience of problem-finding and -solving is the practitioners'.

In other words, "the action research needs to aim at two things simultaneously: (a) to produce evidence needed to solve practical problems; and (b) to help those who are doing the action research to acquire more adequate perspective regarding their problems, to deepen their insights as to what is involved in their task, and to extend their orientation toward . . . what is significant in . . . " teaching-learning.[8]

One critical ingredient of this sort of approach is a realization that the sharing, as a full partner, in such an experience adds immensely to the development of the participants, of their self-esteem, insight, competence, and autonomy.[9] Moreover, without their contribution, there is little hope of any

[6] Nevitt Sanford. "Whatever Happened to Action Research?" *Journal of Social Issues* 26: 3-23; Autumn 1970.

[7] Margaret Mead. As quoted by Karen Schaar in: "Mead, Bronfenbrenner Critique Family Research." *American Psychological Association Monitor* 6: 8; May 1975.

[8] Hilda Taba and Elizabeth Noel. *Action Research: A Case Study.* Washington, D.C.: Association for Supervision and Curriculum Development, 1957. p. 2. Also see the 1957 ASCD Yearbook, *Research for Curriculum Improvement.*

[9] Nevitt Sanford, "Whatever Happened to Action Research?" *op. cit.* Parallel examples in therapy and education may be found in sources like: Virginia M. Axline. *Play Therapy.* New York: Ballantine Books, Inc., 1969; George Dennison. *The Lives of Children.* New York: Vintage Books, 1969; Shepard Ginandes. *The School We Have.* New York: Dell Publishing Co., Inc., 1973; Clark Moustakas. *Teaching as Learning.* New York: Ballantine Books, Inc., 1972; A.S. Neill. *Summerhill.* New York: Hart Publishing Company, Inc., 1960; and Arlene Uslander, Caroline Weiss, Judith Telman, and Esona Wernick. *Their Universe.* New York: Dell Publishing Co., Inc., 1974.

appreciable educational innovations in school or elsewhere. Thus, for example, it has been said of curriculum reform movements that:

. . . unless teachers are accorded full intellectual partnership in both the substance and pedagogy of what they are expected to teach, new sequences of materials, no matter how elegantly contrived, will introduce disappointingly few youngsters to the inherent pleasure of learning. Not only intriguing programs are required but also live models of the inquiring scholar with whom students can identify.[10]

## In Context

Another ingredient of importance is an appreciation of the complex nature of human interactions in which "everything is cause to everything else." In this process of "circular causation," "if one condition changes other conditions will change in response, and those secondary changes in their turn cause new changes all around, and so forth. The conditions and their changes are thus interdependent."[11] Understanding of such involved dynamics is seldom possible from a reductionistic stance and an *in vitro* frame of reference. Without an intimate knowledge of a particular situation with its unique combinations of conditions, and without asking questions that are significant *in vivo*, one rarely arrives at a viable next step in the continuous exploration, as well as in the development of the interested parties.

The interdependence of factors precludes a compartmentalized approach that focuses on a part to neglect the whole. Thus, "to understand the events that occur in social interactions one must comprehend the interplay of these events with the broader social context in which they occur."[12]

Take the example of the children of certain Native American heritages. Their "incomprehensible" behavior and performance in school have, in many instances, led to teacher consternation, exasperation, and hostility. The "fact" in isolation may indeed be that the young ones avoid direct eye contacts with the teacher, are reluctant to talk in front of their classmates, or withdraw from group participation and competition. However, this figure, when placed against the proper ground, tends to reveal that these children learn in their own style, which contrasts sharply with that of most Anglo children. With the full support of their community and family, they watch to learn, participate on their own terms, test themselves privately, develop mental competence, and finally proceed to actual physical performance. In

---

[10] Robert J. Schaefer. *The School as a Center of Inquiry.* New York: Harper & Row, Publishers, 1967. p. 52. Also see: Seymour B. Sarason. *The Culture of the School and the Problem of Change.* Boston: Allyn and Bacon, Inc., 1971.

[11] Gunnar Myrdal. "The Unity of the Social Sciences." *Human Organization* 34: 328; Winter 1975.

[12] Morton Deutsch. "On Making Social Psychology More Useful." *Social Science Research Council Items* 30: 5; March 1976.

the face of the intrusion of a structurally and culturally alien schooling system, they remain consistent with themselves only to suffer the labeling of mental retardation, learning handicaps, or personality disturbance.[13] The imposition of the life style of the dominant subculture seldom leads to the desired sharing and broadening of human and humane perspective. Many teachers and administrators should certainly heed the admonition given by an old and wise canon to a young missionary going off on his first assignment: "Don't be sorry for yourself because you are going to so remote a parish. Be sorry for the Indians. You know nothing and they must teach you."[14]

The need for contextual observation, interpretation, and understanding can readily be seen in such an area of concern as the school experience of children in relation to their class and ethnic background. Here also, a simple-minded expectation of unfavorable self-image in poor and/or minority students, or of their higher academic achievement in desegregated schools, is likely to be discarded for a more complex view of the individual figures nested in a collective field.[15] For example, to be a black child from a close nuclear family of the middle class in a predominantly white community, attending a predominantly white, desegregated school, would be a radically different experience than that of a black child from a close extended family of the working class in a predominantly black community, attending a predominantly black, desegregated school. Each of these and other multitudinous combinations of the numerous factors involved would represent a different life space for a given child, a life space difficult to fathom without the active participation of the child himself or herself.

In the case of bilinguals, as a final example, the picture is no less intricate. Both the learner's aptitudes and motivation-attitudes appear to influence the process of the bilingual learning, but not the same facets. Thus, among the English-Canadian students learning French, it was reported that, although the aptitude variables are important in learning the language skills emphasized in school, for example, grammar, they play little part in the development of the skills of active usage, for example, accuracy of pronunciation and auditory comprehension. The latter was largely a correlate of the integrative, as contrasted with instrumental, motivation to learn French. A learner's

[13]Courtney B. Cazden. *Child Language and Education.* New York: Holt, Rinehart and Winston, Inc., 1972; Edward T. Hall. *The Silent Language.* Garden City, New York: Doubleday & Company, Inc., 1959.

[14]Margaret Craven. *I Heard the Owl Call My Name.* New York: Doubleday & Company, Inc., 1974. p. 12.

[15] Jules Henry. *Jules Henry on Education.* New York: Vintage Books, 1972; Morris Rosenberg and Roberta G. Simmons. *Black and White Self-Esteem: The Urban School Child.* Washington, D.C.: American Sociological Association, n.d.

orientation is instrumental when the overriding concern for language learning is utilitarian, while it is integrative when the learner is primarily interested in understanding the language community and its culture. Moreover, these two outlooks seem to reflect the basic orientations of the student's family, regardless of the actual level of parental language skills or the extent of their cross-community contacts. In other words, these are general attitudinal dispositions that are not specific to any particular language or group of people.[16]

This whole dynamics is further complicated by the still broader social context of intercultural relations.[17] Where two peoples meet, there typically is found a power-status differential that also reflects on the two languages. Given a dichotomy of dominance-nondominance on each of the three factors, that is, the teacher, learner, and language, one readily derives eight variations in the instructional interactions. If, for instance, a teacher from the dominant subculture is teaching the dominant language to a group of students of the nondominant subculture, the situation is very different from when a nondominant teacher is teaching a nondominant language to dominant students. Most of these combinations have not even been considered as a possibility, and little systematic attempt has been made to unravel the vital enigma.

The case, throughout, is of people acting and interacting in context, striving for control of their own fate and for meaning in their life. Research, as a human enterprise, must study, learn from, and be of help to them in this quest. Multicultural education offers us a particularly poignant challenge and opportunity.

---

[16] Wallace E. Lambert. "A Social Psychology of Bilingualism." *Journal of Social Issues* 23: 91-109; April 1967.

[17] Courtney B. Cazden, *Child Language and Education, op. cit.;* Joyce O. Hertzler. *A Sociology of Language.* New York: Random House, Inc., 1965.

# 12

# Curriculum Design for Multicultural Education

Geneva Gay

The process of curriculum development in and of itself is a complex, unceasing, and often frustrating task. It becomes even more difficult when the discipline or subject area to which it is to be applied is relatively new, still emerging, and one whose philosophical articulation is not clearly definitive. Such is the case with multicultural education. Yet, it is imperative that sound multicultural education curricula be developed if the concept is to be effectively translated from theory to practice, and is to become an operational dimension of the programmatic activities of American schools. The difficulty of the task does not, in any way, lessen its importance. If anything it intensifies the need and illuminates a fundamental weakness in the development of multicultural education to date: that is, the absence of the use of systematic approaches or design strategies in most of the multicultural or ethnic studies programs that have been produced so far.

Invariably, these programs have resulted from trial and error experimentation, with little or no attention given to the principles and comprehensive processes of curriculum development. The times now demand that we cease using haphazard, fragmentary approaches in creating multicultural education programs, and develop systematic plans for instruction instead. It will be virtually impossible for such programs to command academic respect if their formulation ignores the acceptable principles of curriculum design. And without this respect the acceptability of the programs within the educational community is diminished considerably.

Educators agree that curriculum development is a systematic procedure, but not necessarily a rigidly sequential one, which involves at least five clearly discernible steps. These include an assessment or diagnosis of needs; the identification of general aims and specific objectives; the selection and organization of content; the determination of learning experiences and teaching strategies; and a program for evaluating student learnings. Each aspect of the process has several different components which combine to form a functional set of interrelated activities that, when applied to the act of selecting and ordering educational experiences, constitutes curriculum construction.

If this process is universally applicable to organizing subject matter content and learning experiences into logical plans for instruction, then it should be usable in designing curriculum for multicultural education. Using an organizational schema or frame of reference that educators are generally familiar with to translate such a difficult concept into practice may facilitate the understanding of the concept, and the development and implementation of more valid, coherent, and comprehensive multicultural education programs. Thus, curriculum design for multicultural education must, of necessity, involve decisions about objectives to be achieved, content to be included, ways of organizing the content, selecting types of learning experiences, and evaluating student learnings.

A detailed discussion of each of these curriculum development components is beyond the scope of this paper. We will focus instead on identifying objectives and organizing content. Assuredly, the process of developing multicultural curriculum would be more comprehensible if each step were delineated in detail. However, incomplete as it is, a discussion of objectives and content is still useful and credible, for it can begin to provide some structure and order to the process of replacing the hodgepodge collection of poorly conceptualized programs now called ethnic studies and/or multicultural education with better planned ones.

## Philosophy of Multicultural Education

A clearly articulated philosophy of multicultural education is essential to expediting the curriculum development process. It provides a conceptual frame of reference and a focus or direction from which objectives, materials, and learning activities are derived. It offers theoretical statements as to what is multicultural education and why it should be a part of school programs. The knowledge, understandings, attitudes, and skills which constitute the substance of multicultural education are implied in the statement of philosophy.

The philosophy of multicultural education suggests that ethnic diversity

and cultural pluralism should be essential ingredients and unceasing characteristics of American education. Their essentiality in educational experiences
is paramount because the demands of living effectively as functional citizens
in a culturally pluralistic society dictate that students learn to know and
appreciate different ethnic groups and their life styles. Schools are socializing
agencies and, as such, they should prepare students to truly accept cultural
and ethnic diversity as normative and valuative to American society. This
means acquiring accurate knowledge and developing positive attitudes about
a variety of different ethnic groups, their histories, cultural heritages, life
styles, and value systems. It means accepting the *right* of different ethnic
groups to exist; understanding the validity and viability of ethnic groups' life
styles as functional cultural entities; maximizing individuals' abilities to
function in their own ethnic communities and others as well; and promoting
the preservation of ethnic and cultural differences as a means of maintaining
the richness and greatness of American society.

School curricula which do not include multicultural content and multiethnic perspectives in teaching are unrealistic and incapable of providing
qualitative educational experiences for all American youths. Such curricula
ignore the fact that ethnic and cultural differences have always been a part of
American life. Most immigrants and American Indian groups have not been
completely assimilated or acculturated into the behavioral styles and value
systems prescribed by Anglo-Saxons, and which dominate mainstream society. Rather, they have preserved their separate ethnic identities and maintained much of their original cultural traditions and/or developed somewhat
modified ones. They have made, and continue to make, valuable contributions to the development of America and the advancement of humankind.
Moreover, ethnic group identity and background experiences influence students' behavioral patterns, value systems, expectations, and learning styles.
These are often in conflict with school expectations and mainstream society's
conceptions of normality. Too frequently those ethnic groups which are the
most different culturally and racially from the dominant society are subjected
to discrimination, racism, stereotyping, isolation, and stigmatization.

Embedded in these realities are implications for redesigning and revitaliz-
ing all aspects of schooling. Curriculum designs for multicultural education
can serve as a means to broad general educational reforms. These designs
should include the facts and effects of cultural pluralism in learning experiences. The information and experiences which constitute multicultural curricula must be valid, comprehensive, and comprehensible. This means including content about a wide variety of ethnic groups that is accurate and
authentic, interdisciplinary, cognitive and affective, multidimensional, and
systematically organized. Objectives must be clearly defined, practical, and
attainable. Learning activities must be realistic, academically sound, and

capable of facilitating students' understanding of the multifarious, complex nature of cultural pluralism and ethnic diversity within the context of American history and culture. These curriculum designs must be created to serve all children in all grades, regardless of their ethnic identity.

## General Objectives

Multicultural curriculum designs should include both general and specific, or performance, objectives. Specific multicultural objectives are relativistic in that they are determined by the needs of the populations to be served and the focus or emphases of particular programs. The kinds of multicultural education programs and the behavioral objectives possible for each are too numerous to attempt a description here. A more plausible approach is to discuss some of the general aims and purposes of multicultural education. These can be categorized according to the knowledge, attitudes, and skills to be learned.

A prime objective of multicultural education is to correct ethnic and racial myths and stereotypes by providing students with accurate information on the histories, lives, and cultures of ethnic groups. Too often school curricula have omitted blacks, Puerto Ricans, American Indians, Cubans, Mexican Americans, and Asian Americans entirely, or depicted them in negative ways. Multicultural curricula can correct these distortions by explaining the contributions these minorities have made to American history and culture, and by presenting honest, comprehensive portrayals of their life experiences. This means including information about their status in American society in contemporary and historical perspective and their characteristics as functional cultural entities, as well as their contributions.

Another purpose of multicultural education is to correct the mistaken notion that an ethnic group is synonymous with a minority group. There are both majority and minority ethnic groups, and both kinds should be included in multicultural curricula. Such groups as Italian Americans, Polish Americans, Jews, and German Americans should be included in the curriculum along with blacks, Latinos, American Indians, and Asian Americans. Thus, the curriculum should allow for students to study a wide variety of different kinds of ethnic groups so that they can better understand the complexity and saliency of ethnicity in the lives of individuals and groups, and the viability of alternative life styles.

We are all members of ethnic groups. Yet we know little about our own and others' ethnicity. We do not know and understand the facts about how ethnic experiences affect our behavior and values and our concepts of self-identity, or the particulars of different ethnic groups' contributions and historical experiences. If asked, most of us would be hard pressed to give more than a few bits and pieces of information about even the most noticeable ethnic groups. Even this information is likely to be skewed or distorted because school curricula to date have failed to encourage the comprehensive study of different ethnic groups in America. Nor do we clearly understand how and why some ethnic groups have been victimized by powerlessness, racism, discrimination, alienation, and isolation while others have benefited from having access to the economic, social, and political institutions and reward systems. Therefore, another purpose of multicultural curriculum is to help students develop ethnic literacy by filling these cognitive voids.

Knowledge objectives are necessary but insufficient to design sound, comprehensive multicultural education experiences. Students also need to be exposed to content and learning activities that will facilitate the development of attitudes and values conducive to the preservation and promotion of ethnic and cultural diversity as a positive quality of society. Included among the attitudinal objectives are enhancing students' self-concepts by developing pride in one's own and others' ethnic and cultural heritages, and increasing one's sense of cultural identity and ethnic unity. Multicultural curriculum can thus serve both to confirm one's own ethnicity and human worth, and to validate other ethnic groups' life styles. The curriculum should also aim to help students develop openness, flexibility, and receptivity to cultural diversity and alternative life styles; enrich human experiences through the study of different ethnic groups; accept and prize diversity; and reduce anxieties about encountering different ethnic groups, their life styles, value preferences, and behavioral patterns. These should all be major objectives of multicultural education programs because decision making and social participation in culturally pluralistic settings involve knowledge, values, and skills.

The third category of objectives which combine with knowledge and attitudes to comprise the broad construct of objectives for multicultural education is skills. A curriculum which does not include the development of skills that will increase and enhance students' capabilities to live and function in culturally pluralistic settings is incomplete. Constructive change requires action. Responsible action requires knowledge, values, and skills. Therefore, if students are to change their perceptions about ethnically, racially, and culturally different people they must become actively involved in a behavior modification process. One of the skills needed is introspection and reflective self-analysis. This is a requisite to clarifying one's own racial and ethnic attitudes and values. Students must be taught how to make responsible decisions and how to gain, maintain, and exercise political power, so that they can resolve personal problems, increase their political efficacy, and influence public policy as it relates to ethnic diversity and cultural pluralism. Multicultural curriculum must also include learning experiences which are designed to improve students' skills in cross-cultural communication. Learning how to eliminate the debilitating effects of discrimination and racism and how to offset the psychologically incapacitating effects of stereotyping is contingent upon students knowing how racist practices operate and having access to historically accurate knowledge and authentic experiences with ethnic groups that capture the essence of their cultural traditions and existential conditions in American life.

## Organizing Multicultural Content

To a large extent the kind of objectives identified for multicultural education and how they are prioritized dictate the selection and organization of the content to be included in the curriculum. Despite this fact, and for the sake of comprehensiveness and authenticity, content which addresses the many different dimensions or components of the lives of ethnic group members must be included in multicultural curricula. This includes content on a wide variety of majority and minority ethnic groups, their cultural characteristics and value systems, intra-ethnic group variations, current status in society, the conditions of their political, economic, and social existence in historical perspective, and their contributions to the advancement of humankind.

There are several different strategies for selecting and organizing multicultural content into manageable and plausible plans of instruction. These include adding ethnic content to existing curricula, a modified skills design, a problems approach, a thematic approach, and a conceptual framework approach. None of these is a panacea for all the problems of implementing multicultural education, but each has the potential for providing some structure and focus to the process of developing defensible curriculum designs.

Probably the easiest, the oldest, and the most frequently used approaches are to add factual information about ethnic groups to the different subject matter disciplines taught in the schools, and to create separate units or courses on specific ethnic groups. More often than not the ethnic groups have been minorities, the disciplines affected have been secondary social studies and language arts, and the content has been limited to ethnic contributions. These strategies are the least promising because they are fragmentary and contrary to the philosophy that multicultural education should be broadly conceptualized to include both minority and majority ethnic groups, comprehensive in the treatment of ethnic group life experiences, and permeate all learning experiences of all children.

Similarly, the problems approach to multicultural curriculum design is too limited in scope and conceptualization to meet all the criteria of multicultural education. The focus of attention is the social, economic, and political problems ethnic groups encounter within American society. This approach to designing multicultural curriculum has an inherent quality of negativism embedded in it. It is easily susceptible to perpetuating distortions about ethnicity and ethnic groups, for ethnicity becomes analogous to "problems" or "something negative," while ethnic groups are equated to minorities. Such issues as political powerlessness, poor housing, unemployment, illiteracy, and crime as they relate to ethnic groups are catchwords of the curriculum. And, multicultural education comes to be the study of "the Negro problem," "the Indian problem," "the Cuban problem," and "the Asian problem." While it is important for students to examine societal problems ethnic groups encounter, for the curriculum to focus exclusively on them is to do injustice to the concept of multicultural education. Rather than developing pride in one's ethnic heritages and appreciation for those of others, such curricula are likely to do the reverse. They are also likely to develop patronizing and condescending attitudes in students who consider themselves among the "advantaged" toward the "problem ethnic groups."

A more plausible curriculum design strategy is to modify the approach used to teach basic academic skills. It is based on the premise that ethnically relevant content, techniques, and perspectives should be used to teach such fundamental skills as reading, writing, arithmetic, and reasoning as well as the conceptual skills specific to different disciplines. It further suggests that the idea of "basic skills" should be broadened to include social participation, cross-cultural communication and functioning, decision making, and reflective self-analysis, since proficiency in these areas is essential to living successfully in our pluralistic society. The basic skills form the core of the curriculum design and a variety of ethnically specific materials are selected as the means or vehicles through which these skills are taught. Ethnic storybooks for children have as much potential for teaching some reading skills as do basal readers. Novels, plays, poems, and essays written by and about blacks, Italian Americans, Jewish Americans, Puerto Rican Americans, and Japanese Americans are as useful in teaching literary techniques and criteria of quality literature as are writings by and about Anglo Americans. Such content has the additional advantage of introducing students to the lives of different ethnic groups through their own literary writings.

The music of blacks, Cubans, and Poles possesses all the attributes necessary to teach students the technical components of music and music appreciation, as well as offering an introduction to the unique techniques and qualities of specific types of ethnic music. The sciences and mathematics can be made more personable and interesting by including the contributions different ethnic individuals have made to these fields of knowledge. Economic, political, and social situations or events involving different ethnic groups, such as the march on Washington, the Boston busing controversy, the lettuce boycott, the Wounded Knee affair, and the Kanawha County book crisis, can be used to develop student abilities in rational analysis, values clarification, decision making, and social activism. The possibility of students mastering these basic skills is maximized because the content used in teaching them is pertinent to their life experiences, and the instructional techniques are more compatible with their value systems and learning styles.

The two curriculum design strategies which seem to be most capable of meeting all the criteria of multicultural education are the thematic approach and the conceptual framework design. The knowledge explosion applies as much to the fields of ethnic diversity and cultural pluralism as to other disciplines. As scholastic research continues and more factual information becomes available on ethnic groups, the likelihood of students being able to comprehend it all diminishes considerably. And even if they could, mere memorization of facts and chronology about ethnic groups is insufficient to develop ethnic literacy and acceptance of the vitality of ethnicity in American society. Students must have some ways of processing this mass of information in a context that is meaningful and manageable. The thematic approach to curriculum development offers such a device.

The human condition, the social realities of American life, and the experiences of ethnic group members are characterized by unceasing concerns with certain issues having to do with personal development and improving the quality of life. These themes or issues are universal in that they apply to all ethnic groups, and recurrent because they appear repeatedly throughout the growth and development of ethnic groups' histories and cultures. Examples of these recurrent universal themes are: Who am I?, or a search for identity; struggle for survival; preservation and enhancement of human dignity; struggle for freedom; justice and equality for all; cultural articulation; and the presence and influence of different ethnic groups in all aspects of American life, history, and culture. This list is not exhaustive, but merely illustrative of the kind of themes that can be identified.

Using the thematic approach to curriculum design allows for a multitude of materials, experiences, and techniques to be interwoven into multicultural education programs. Understanding the complex multifarious nature of each of the themes requires the use of knowledge, concepts, and principles from many different disciplines. Thus, interdisciplinary techniques, comparative analyses, and multiethnic perspectives are necessary in examining each theme to determine what it means to different ethnic groups, how they have responded to it, and to ascertain others' reactions to their responses. For students to adequately explore ethnic groups' search for identity they will have to examine the ideologies, values, behaviors, and communications of each. This will mean studying their philosophy, literature, language, folklore, psychology, history, sociology, and music. Ethnic groups' struggle for survival includes physical, economic, cultural, political, and psychological dimensions. To comprehend the complexity of the issue requires students to determine what constitutes "survival" for different ethnic groups, how its component parts are prioritized, and to understand how these decisions reflect values and affect behaviors. Developing the theme that different ethnic groups have always been present on the American scene and influential in shaping the character of American life and culture entails using multiethnic perspectives and multicultural content to explore, among other things, the country's military battles, political campaigns, industrial growth, scientific achievements, and leisure activities.

Another useful technique for designing multicultural curriculum to better manage the explosion of knowledge on ethnic groups is to use a conceptual framework as the guiding principle for organizing content. Learning experiences are organized around a series of generic concepts selected from different disciplines and applicable to all ethnic group experiences. These might include such concepts as power, ethnicity, unity within diversity, culture, socialization, racism, alienation, assimilation, and morality. Others can be selected from the social sciences, the behavioral sciences, linguistics and communication, and philosophy.

In addition to identifying a series of generic concepts the conceptual framework approach to multicultural curriculum development involves selecting specific supportive concepts for each generic concept; listing major and minor generalizations derived from the concepts; identifying general and performance objectives for each concept; and selecting appropriate multicultural content, learning experiences, and instructional strategies to teach the concepts. It too lends itself easily to such instructional techniques as multiethnic perspectives, interdisciplinary approaches, and comparative analyses. Students are instructed in applied concept mastery in that concepts are studied from the vantage point of the perspectives and experiences of different ethnic groups instead of as abstract principles. To engage in these academic exercises students will have to use a number of different skills simultaneously. They must have some knowledge about the meaning of the concept itself and about its contextual meaning in relation to ethnic group experiences; be capable of using inquiry skills to collect data from a variety of different sources; have the ability to clarify their racial and ethnic attitudes and values; and be able to make rational decisions. For example, understanding the concept of power within the context of ethnicity means analyzing it from the historical and contemporary political, sociological, and economic perspectives and experiences of a wide variety of ethnic groups. It also means examining reasons that some ethnic groups have access to power while others do not, how the access to or lack of power affects the civic and social attitudes and behaviors of groups and individuals, and exploring ways of acquiring and exercising economic and political power. This conception of interdependence is as much a biological, sociological, economic, political, and anthropological issue as it is a psychological and a historical one.

Comprehending the complex concepts of culture and ethnicity is indispensable to understanding the dynamics of ethnic diversity and cultural plural-ism in American society. It requires defining each one in both theoretical and behavioral terms. It involves extricating from among the generic components of American culture those which are unique to different ethnic groups. Such aspects of ethnic groups' cultures as value systems, communication styles, behavioral patterns, and socialization processes must be identified and examined. The curriculum content is selected from the writings, traditions, customs, myths and oral histories, religion, arts, music, and language of the ethnic groups, and from empirical research data gathered by social and behavioral scientists. Thus, the content and techniques of such disciplines as the social sciences, natural sciences, fine arts, folklore, history, the behavioral sciences, and socio/psycho-linguistics are essential to teaching the concepts of ethnicity and culture.

## Conclusion

Curriculum development for multicultural education is no easy task. Its difficulty is compounded by the fact that there are relatively few educators adequately prepared to undertake or supervise the task. Before we can expect to have respectable multicultural curriculum designs which are based on sound academic principles we must prepare or train those school personnel who are assigned the responsibility of developing curricula in the particulars of ethnic and cultural differences. For, as the adage goes, "You can't teach what you don't know." Nor can you design what you don't understand.

The ideas for designing multicultural curricula discussed herein are of-fered as feasible suggestions that can expedite the process by providing a frame of reference, a focus or direction, a starting point. They are not without faults. Nor are they dogmatic dicta. And there is no guarantee that even if each were followed religiously they would result in effective multicultural education programs. After all, curriculum development is only one piece of the educational pie, and it must be seen and accepted as such with all the limitations inherent in that. Instruction, administration, staff development and teacher education, and school climate are equally as important as curric-ulum in implementing comprehensive educational reforms designed to be responsive to the dictates of cultural pluralism and ethnic diversity.

Undoubtedly, many educators will choose not to accept any of the sugges-tions offered herein, and will chart their own courses of action. That is per-fectly all right and is even encouraged. However, whatever strategies are employed in developing multicultural curriculum designs it is absolutely es-sential that the basic components of curriculum development be included — that is, establishing a rationale or philosophy of multicultural education, identifying objectives, assessing needs, selecting and organizing content and learning experiences, and evaluating student learnings. Instructional plans which do not include these components cannot presume to be curriculum. The concept of multicultural education can no longer afford to have fragmentary, poorly conceptualized units of instruction masquerading as realistic curriculum designs.

# 13

# Developing Multicultural Learning Activities

H. Prentice Baptiste, Jr., and Mira Baptiste

During very recent years the relationship between cultural pluralism and multicultural education has been questioned by educators on numerous occasions. This is a very complex concept which raises difficult questions. The search for curriculum materials reflective of cultural pluralism is demanding. Establishing criteria for evaluation of curriculum materials, utilization of existing local resources, identification of subject integrating concepts, and formulation of guidelines for implementation of the multicultural processes are examples of this complex multifaceted problem.

## Complexity of Multicultural Processes

Cultural pluralism has been defined from many vantage points that reflect various areas of concern, ranging, for example, from the national government to the smallest school district. Whatever the area of concern, underlying the definition of cultural pluralism is a philosophy that strongly recommends a particular set of beliefs, principles, and ideas that should govern the relationship of people of diverse cultures. The cornerstone principles of cultural pluralism are equality, mutual acceptance and understanding, and a sense of moral commitment. Equality in cultural pluralism does not mean the assignment of percentage and ratio opportunity chances for certain individuals or particular groups. Equality in the context of cultural pluralism is the antithesis of racism, prejudice, oppression, and assigned percentage opportunity of chances.

Another fundamental principle of cultural pluralism is the mutual acceptance and understanding of cultural diversity. Groups as well as individuals must learn that diversity, not uniformity or sameness, is the order of the day. As Carlos Cortés explains, knowledge is not equivalent to understanding.[1] Knowledge of cultural groups does not guarantee understanding. Subsequently, creative instructional strategies along with valid materials must be utilized to facilitate understanding.

Multicultural education is the process of institutionalizing the philosophy of cultural pluralism within education systems. This is not an easy process. As Tomás Arciniega has stated, "The issue of moving schools and universities toward a culturally pluralistic state may appear, to some, to be a simple matter. The fact is, however, that the thrust toward achieving cultural pluralism in educational form and practice is a complex and value-laden undertaking."[2]

As one develops the multicultural processes within an elementary and secondary school, he/she is confronted with traditional obstacles like the monocultural process of the assimilation or the melting pot philosophy, unequal availability of educational opportunities, hostility or disregard for diversity, racism, and prejudice which mitigate against its implementation. However, proponents of multicultural processes must affirm the ethical commitment of schools to the aforementioned principles of cultural pluralism.

The multicultural process is not an add on to existing educational programs. It does not mean studying certain minority groups, for example, Native Americans, or Japanese Americans, from two o'clock to three o'clock on Mondays and Wednesdays. The studying of Mexican American literature in isolation from the American literature course implies a certain illegitimacy about Mexican American literature. Mexican American literature, as well as the literature of other ethnic groups, has a legitimate place in the regular American literature course. Bilingual programs which are based on a transitional model, that is, elimination of instruction in mother tongue as soon as second language acquisition occurs, are not representative of the multicultural process. Language curricular activities which neglect the cultural value systems of the languages are detrimental to formation of valid instructional activities. Educators who tend to utilize only special ethnic holidays, religious ceremonials, super-heroes, and foods to culturalize their instruction are

---

[1]Carlos Cortés. "Understanding Not Tolerance." Portion of a videotape entitled: *Perspectives on Multicultural Education.* Developed by H. Prentice Baptiste, Jr., 1976.

[2]Tomás A. Arciniega. "The Thrust Toward Pluralism: What Progress?" *Educational Leadership* 33 (3): 163; December 1975.

being dreadfully shortsighted. Furthermore, they are miseducating our youth to the real values of various cultural and ethnic groups.

## The Quest for Materials

Numerous instructional materials contain subtleties of velvet racism, sexism, and stereotypes, and are supportive of the assimilationist philosophy. As Banks has indicated, most materials are insensitive, inaccurate, and written from an Anglo-Saxon perspective.[3] Several guidelines have been suggested elsewhere which provide criteria to facilitate selection of good materials.[4] However, many teachers must face the reality that they will have to utilize available materials and resources from their school district to supplement their instructional strategies. Nevertheless, inaccurate, insensitive, stereotypic materials need not provide an impassable obstacle to knowledgeable multicultural-oriented teachers. Especially is this credible if one believes the teacher is the curriculum.[5]

The quest for multicultural materials often leads one to commercial materials; but it appears that the companies which produce educational materials do not believe a market exists for such. On the other hand, some companies do believe a market exists, but are reluctant to develop materials because of the complex nature of such a national endeavor. Companies prepare educational materials for national markets and are not responsive to local concerns. The market has been flooded with numerous ethnic materials which usually have as their focus a specific ethnic group; but the need exists for materials which include a diversity of ethnic groups.

The feasibility of producing materials representative of all ethnic groups may not be resolved. The Institute of Texas Cultures in its attempt to produce materials about all groups who settled Texas is working on its 26th group.[6] In Pennsylvania, an agency has been formed at Bloomsburg State

[3]James A. Banks. "Evaluating and Selecting Ethnic Studies Materials." *Educational Leadership* 33 (7): 593; April 1974.

[4]"The ABC's of Freeing Day Care From Racism, Sexism." *Interracial Books for Children Bulletin.* Vol. 6, Nos. 5 & 6. New York, N.Y.: Council on Interracial Books for Children; Gloria Grant. "Criteria for Cultural Pluralism in the Classroom." *Educational Leadership* 32 (3): December 1974; Task Force on Racism and Bias in the Teaching of English. "Criteria for Teaching Materials in Reading and Literature." Urbana, Illinois: National Council of Teachers of English; Max Rosenberg. "Evaluate Your Textbooks for Racism, Sexism!" *Educational Leadership* 31 (2): 108-109; November 1973; Maxine Dunfee. "Curriculum Materials for Celebrating the Bicentennial." *Educational Leadership* 33 (4): 267-72; January 1976.

[5]Milo Kalectaca, Gerald Knowles, and Robin Butterfield. "To Help — Not To Homogenize Native American Children." *Educational Leadership* 31 (7): 592; April 1974.

[6]*People* 5; September-October 1975. Published by Institute of Texan Cultures, San Antonio, Texas.

College to identify the various ethnic groups in that state.[7] This agency is also charged with identification, location, and development of instructional materials on ethnic groups within the state of Pennsylvania. Frequently, the catalyst for the development of clearinghouses on ethnic materials has been provided by federal funds. Efforts have centered on the identification of ethnic groups within a specific geographic region or unit such as a state. This has led to an identification of additional resources and the development of instructional materials. Productions of this sort are limited by several specifics: namely, geographic area involved, peoples contributing to this area, and available historical background information. Monies received by states for desegregation purposes have produced agencies such as The Center for Public School Ethnic Studies in Texas.[8]

The zealous effort to produce numerous ethnic materials is not totally good for culturally pluralizing educational programs. In many instances the quality of numerous ethnic materials tends to perpetuate or create erroneous myths, stereotypes, and pseudo super-heroes. No controls exist to ensure the purchaser/user of the authenticity of these materials. The user tends to over-indulge in another myth by seeking a member of the group under study to verify the authenticity of the materials.

Ethnic materials per se tend to create a monoethnic or mono approach. Although it is understood that ethnic materials as well as certain ethnic experiences must be viewed in a multicultural program, nonetheless instruction must not end at this point. The teacher must bring about the multicultural processes via instructional strategies. He/she must serve as a cultural engineer to effectively utilize monoethnic materials.

As one utilizes ethnic materials, he/she must be aware that some of these materials may contain examples of velvet racism and stereotypes. Another problem with some ethnic materials is the creation of new unfounded myths. Apparently the heroic nature of our "common culture" is encouraging the creation of numerous ethnic super-heroes. Many of these super-heroes are crumbling because there is little or no substantial evidence except mythology to support their deeds. Conflicting information characterizes too much of this material. Several materials relating the same event may contain not only opposing views, but also conflicting facts. Granted, some conflict is expected between interethnic materials; but the conflict referred to here is that produced by shoddy research regarding the event, the place, and/or the group of people.

[7]Pennsylvania Ethnic Heritage Studies Dissemination Project, Bloomsburg State College, Bloomsburg, Pennsylvania.

[8]Center for Public School Ethnic Studies, Extension Building, The University of Texas, Austin, Texas.

## Efforts To Provide Materials

Through the efforts of HEW's Ethnic Heritage Studies, ESEA and ESAA ethnic material resources on a national level are being identified, developed, and evaluated. AACTE has established a clearinghouse for the collection and evaluation of multicultural materials. Teacher Corps projects have for several years been involved in the development of multicultural materials.

Several states are facilitating, through coordination and provision of funds, the development, location, and dissemination of materials for multicultural education. As mentioned earlier, some states are specifically coordinating the identification, development, and dissemination of materials about cultural/ethnic groups within their borders. Interested educators can contact their state education agency for information in regard to the efforts of their state in this endeavor.

Teachers are usually quite surprised when referred to local resources for materials that will facilitate the multicultural processes. The local community is often a rich reservoir of materials. Historical information about the contributions of various cultural/ethnic groups within a community are usually available. Other primary resources within a community are the people themselves, business and industry, professions, and local education agencies.

Special interest groups or agencies within a community have ethnic/cultural and/or multicultural materials. These groups, for example, the Anti-Defamation League, American Red Cross, and French Speaking Union, will make available to teachers ethnic and also multicultural materials. In the latter category, the American Red Cross has a film — "Blood Is Life, Pass It On" — which is an excellent example of a good multicultural film. Usually, materials from community special interest groups are free or available at a nominal cost. Special interest groups tend to disseminate materials that are culturally and ethnically diverse in addition to promoting a culturally pluralistic philosophy.

The local library quite often is disregarded by teachers in their quest for materials, yet one may be surprised at the abundance of materials available for use. In some local communities, libraries are developing annotated bibliographies on available racial, ethnic, and multicultural materials according to grade levels, reading levels, and subject areas. It would be advisable for a teacher interested in "multiculturalizing" classroom instruction to visit the local library. One will also find, for the most part, that these libraries are becoming very sensitive to acquiring materials, that is, books, magazines, films, tapes, which reflect the ethnic/cultural makeup of the local population.

Most school districts have established departments of human relations, ethnic studies, or minority studies, which have as one of their responsibilities the collection, development, dissemination, and evaluation of ethnic/cultural and multicultural materials. In many instances, the staff of these departments, when invited, will come to schools and demonstrate the use of their materials.

## Evaluating and Implementing

Knowing and being able to obtain ethnic/cultural or multicultural materials is only part of the solution. The other part is being able to evaluate the worth of these materials for instructional purposes. Evaluation of existing materials by teachers is of paramount importance. Several guidelines have been published which address only certain facets of multicultural materials. As an example, *Educational Leadership* published a set of guidelines to evaluate the inclusion of treatment of minorities in books and other curriculum materials.[9] Other guidelines have appeared which focus on racism or sexism.[10] Common attributes of most guidelines are an overall negativism and narrowness, which prevent their application to several facets of multicultural materials.

The furore created by community reaction to certain library books and textbooks has moved many school districts to formulate guidelines for instructional materials. The Council on Interracial Books has moved ahead in supplying leadership for groups which need guidelines.

There is no easy way to begin implementation of multicultural learning activities, nor is there a step by step approach. The subject-integrating concept will be used as the first example. The teacher decides upon a concept that may move across subject matter lines, but it must be readily adaptable to the philosophy of cultural pluralism. The teacher may or may not possess adequate knowledge about the concept. The activities and materials must work together. Selection of materials may dictate activities, and implementation of activities could depend heavily upon available materials.

Slavery is a subject-integrating concept which cuts across time lines and cultural/ethnic groups. The phenomenon of slavery is introduced to every school child. Mistakenly, it is usually given as the cause of the Civil War, and most unfortunately it is *the* concept to unveil Afro-Americans. Thus, in the minds of many school children, slavery is linked with Afro-Americans.

Historically, numerous groups of people at one time or another have been slaves or enslavers. Ancient history or modern times offer starting points for this concept. The multicultural process is reflected in an exploration of the

[9]Max Rosenberg, "Evaluate Your Textbooks for Racism, Sexism," *op. cit.*
[10]See n. 4.

slavery concept which involves the use of many groups of people as both slaves and enslavers. A more valid conception of the term can be realized when students are given the opportunity to study slavery from a comparative perspective, which uses the underlying economic structure, religious beliefs, cultural values, and geographic environments.

Teachers have found literature to be a pliable content area, rich in materials and resources. Folktales which include contributions from several groups can be expanded to other subject areas such as music, art, or social studies. Content areas pose very few problems. A creative, sensitive teacher with good competencies in teaching strategies and a working philosophy of cultural pluralism can "multiculturalize" physical education, mathematics, science, art, music, language arts, reading, and even vocational arts. The key question the teacher must answer is "How do I include all peoples who have a rightful place in this lesson?" The teacher is the wheel that turns. The degree of each turn depends upon the teacher's understanding of different ethnic cultures, upon his/her attitudes toward differences in ethnic backgrounds, and upon his/her ability to develop teaching strategies appropriate for the philosophy of cultural pluralism.

Are learning activities in a curriculum reflective of cultural pluralism different from those in a traditional approach? Yes and no. Sound teaching strategies will always involve the students in the process; but multicultural education processes require the materials to illustrate all groups of people as equal, worthy of being, and having dignity. Exclusion is powerful. The absence of peoples, along with the unspoken words, leads students to acquire erroneous information. The teacher faces a double-edged responsibility when materials are chosen. The materials must promote a sense of unity within diversity. Teaching strategies go beyond the memorization of facts to focus on higher levels of knowledge, value analysis, and decision making. The teaching strategies used with the materials can communicate quite effectively the message of cultural pluralism.

The multicultural process includes diversifying the subject matter content as well as humanizing teaching strategies. The teacher should make a constant conscientious effort to create a teaching/learning environment reflective of power sharing, equality, and decision making. It is important for the teacher to realize that shared power and decision making flow in two directions between teacher and students. Designing learning activities which will enable the student to explore his/her self concept is often the beginning stage for the multicultural processes. Self-esteem and worthiness are undeniably linked to the feeling of having some control over one's environment. A real voice in decision making is fundamental for the student to acquire a positive self-esteem. Many subject areas such as art, drama, music, language, social studies, and sociology can be used by teachers to facilitate the positive growth of the students' self-esteem. Content areas are used as exemplars of cultural diversity actualized.

There are no curriculum guides, no material kits, no pre- or post-tests, no objectives, and no teacher editions available for one to plug into the existing courses for "Bingo! Multicultural Education." First and foremost, the teacher must evolve a cultural pluralistic philosophy which emerges as a multicultural experience. The true measure of multicultural education is vested in the behaviors, attitudes, and beliefs of the students. The consequent objective for material effectiveness is evaluated by the teacher not only in terms of students' gains in understandings and knowledge of other people, but in the reduction and resolution of conflicts.

# 14

# Instructional Materials in Multicultural Education

Carl A. Grant and Gloria W. Grant

If printed text materials[1] are viewed as communication devices to help students interpret and respond to their environment, as some have suggested, it would be credible to say that the purpose of instructional materials, especially the textbook, is to transmit culture. Black (1967) supports this premise:

As the most important educational tool of the past and the present, the textbook is instrumental in molding the attitudes and passions of the young and thus both reflects and shapes the beliefs of the nation itself. Indeed, one may suggest that schoolbooks studied by previous generations have had an influence on the development of the American people that is almost as profound as the achievements of Thomas Jefferson, Franklin Delano Roosevelt, and Henry Ford.[2]

Cronbach also noted the importance of the text: "Only the teacher — and perhaps a blackboard and writing materials — are found as universally as the textbook in our classrooms."[3] In his view, the textbook is dominant in the typical school today and marks educational experiences in America from the first grade through college.

Instructional materials are needed to implement educational goals and curricula. They serve as the catalyst for the transformation of concepts from

---

[1] In this paper we discuss printed materials, especially the textbook. However, the scope of this discussion is appropriate to other instructional materials as well.

[2] Hillel Black. *The American Schoolbook*. New York: William Morrow and Company, Inc., 1967. p. 73.

[3] Lee J. Cronbach, editor. *Text Materials in Modern Education*. Urbana, Illinois: University of Illinois Press, 1955. p. 3. Copyright © 1955 by the Board of Trustees of the University of Illinois.

theory into practice. The introduction and implementation of multiculturalism into educational goals and curricula require the use of materials designed to help teachers and students understand and affirm its principles. Therefore, we propose three categories of materials that are essential for successful implementation of multiculturalism into our educational process.

Initially, we will consider teacher awareness materials — materials to help teachers examine their own values, beliefs, prejudices, and attitudes; to acquire basic information about social and institutional norms; and to learn about differences among cultures, races, sexes, ages, and physical sizes and handicaps.[4] Second, we will consider student awareness materials — materials that will help students evaluate their beliefs, values, prejudices, and attitudes; learn basic information about social and institutional norms; and learn about cultural, racial, sex, age, and physical differences. And finally, we will consider classroom materials — materials that will help teachers communicate respect for all children in every classroom in our pluralistic society.

## Teacher Awareness Materials

Unless teachers utilize materials of this first category, as intended, and unless self-awareness and reeducation are undertaken, implementation of multiculturalism into the classroom is destined for ultimate failure. The importance of self-awareness to teaching is well documented in educational literature. Dickeman offers an excellent illustration:

> When teachers begin to recognize that their own ethnic heritages are valuable, that their own family histories are relevant to learning and teaching, the battle is half won. Indeed, I am convinced that without this recognition and acceptance of self, the teacher will remain unable to communicate to his [her] class or to the surrounding community the respect necessary for the creation of contact between life and learning.[5]

Self-awareness should lead to the development of a positive self-image and attitude. Teachers might well consider pertinent materials, such as Jersild's *When Teachers Face Themselves,*[6] to help them explore the nature of their anxieties and biases. Jersild suggests that teacher self-awareness is "the most important requirement" for assisting students in their own self-awareness.

---

[4]Although each person is individually different in his/her own way, the following references to differences in sex, age, physical size, and handicap are grouped as "individual differences."

[5]Mildred Dickeman. "Teaching Cultural Pluralism." James A. Banks, editor. *Teaching Ethnic Studies.* Washington, D.C.: National Council for the Social Studies, 1973. p. 24.

[6]Arthur T. Jersild. *When Teachers Face Themselves.* New York: Teachers College Press, 1955. p. 3.

He concludes that "What is needed is a more personal kind of searching, which will enable the teacher to identify his own concerns and to share the concerns of his students."

Development of self-awareness can be facilitated through the use of materials in dialogue and inquiry sessions,[7] which might provide a mechanism for teachers to better explore the nature of their biases. If these sessions are available and teachers take advantage of them, they will certainly represent a positive approach toward elimination of their prejudices and biases. Our argument here is simply that teachers must first be reeducated in order to understand and respect individuals regardless of their differences, and that this reeducation must begin with themselves.

A part of the reeducation process for teachers should include the studying of materials that examine social and institutional norms in relation to culture, race, age, sex, and physical differences. Materials such as Allport's *The Nature of Prejudice*[8] provide a comprehensive and detailed illustration of the nature of human prejudice and its perpetuation in society and society's institutions.

It is essential that teachers understand that existing social and institutional norms reflect racist, classist, and sexist attitudes and behavior, which continue to prevail in our nation. Concepts that begin as stereotypes often become norms and then the norms are, in turn, manifested in institutional practices. For example, the stereotypes that all blacks are musically inclined and athletic have become norms to many people, and consequently blacks are expected to excel in these areas. Institutions often encourage the stereotype and norm by providing opportunities to blacks in the areas of music and athletics more often than in other professional areas.

One reason for the reeducation process is that most of today's teachers were trained to instruct white middle-class students. Unfortunately, little

---

[7]Dialogue-inquiry is the coordination of two processes: (a) the process whereby two or more persons reveal their feelings and thoughts to one another with a reciprocal awareness of the threat to self-esteem that is involved for each; (b) the process whereby two or more persons ask and answer questions that are relevant to their situation.

In a school, dialogue is a communication among professional colleagues (including parents and students) — a teacher talking to a principal or a problem-solving session of several persons. It is from dialogue, facilitated by the interpersonal competencies of participants, that the specific functions of inquiry (describing and evaluating reality, formulating and analyzing problems, setting goals, elaborating and examining alternative plans, acting to implement a plan for changing reality) are generated and given form and meaning. Dialogue activates inquiry. It enables group members to raise and answer questions and to state and consider alternatives regarding a specific function of inquiry. (By Max R. Goodson. "Dialogue Inquiry." Unpublished notes.) University of Wisconsin-Madison, 1973. p. 3.

[8]Gordon W. Allport. *The Nature of Prejudice.* Garden City, New York: Doubleday & Company, Inc., 1954.

attention was given in preservice training and materials for teaching in a pluralistic society. G. Grant, after an evaluation of teacher training materials, stated,

If the teacher preparation materials examined . . . represent the state of the art of material relative to ethnic and cultural biases and sex role stereotyping, it is clearly evident that teacher preparation materials are inadequate. All of the materials examined need to be corrected before they are used in teacher training institutions. It is disgraceful that we are preparing teachers to teach in a multicultural society using materials that are mostly unicultural.[9]

In addition to acquiring knowledge about themselves and about social and institutional norms, teachers need to build their own libraries or have immediate access to materials on cultural, racial, and individual differences. These materials are often available through private and public, local, regional, and national organizations, such as the Puerto Rican Forum, NAACP, Mexican American Education Association, Anti-Defamation League of B'nai B'rith, Interracial Council on Books, Japanese American Curriculum Project, and the Indian Historical Society. Teachers could begin building their libraries by collecting materials that are representative of the cultural, racial, and individual differences of students in their school or community.

In conjunction with the foregoing materials, appropriate strategies for planned change and teacher ownership must be pursued. Some authorities consider planned change to be a method "which self-consciously and experientially employs social knowledge to help solve the problems of men [and women] and societies."[10] The knowledge of planned change should affect the inclusion of valid and appropriate content in the application of multiculturalism in education. Its function would also assist teachers in developing intelligent and empathetic responses in themselves and in their students. As Bennis *et al.* note:

Men [and women] are guided in their actions by socially funded and communicated meanings, norms, and institutions, in brief by a normative culture. At the personal level, men [and women] are guided by internalized meanings, habits, and values. Changes in patterns of action or practice are, therefore, changes, not alone in the rational information equipment of men [and women], but at the personal level, in habits and values as well and, at the sociocultural level, changes are alterations in

[9]Gloria W. Grant. "Are Today's Teacher Training Materials Preparing Teachers To Teach in a Multi-Cultural Society?" Carl A. Grant, editor. *Sifting and Winnowing: An Exploration of the Relationship Between Multi-Cultural Education and CBTE.* Madison, Wisconsin: Teacher Corps Associates, University of Wisconsin-Madison, 1975. pp. 69-81.

[10]Warren G. Bennis, Kenneth D. Benne, Robert Chin, and Kenneth E. Corey. *The Planning of Change.* New York: Holt, Rinehart & Winston, Inc., 1976.

normative structures and in institutionalizing roles and relationships, as well as in cognitive and perceptual orientations.[11]

In keeping with the strategies for planned change, teachers must have a voice in determining their involvement in educational programs and innovations under consideration. As the current literature on in-service education, teachers centers, and professional organizations attests, teacher ownership has been a neglected area in the educational profession. Grant and Melnick (1976) contend that teachers, for a number of reasons, are not justifiably demanding viable participation in educational programs. "For too long . . . they have not been involved in making decisions that affect their professional growth and the training they need for more successful interaction with students."[12] Teacher involvement and ownership are exceedingly important when implementing a concept such as multiculturalism. As Joyce, Howey, and Yarger[13] (1976) and Mann[14] (1976) report, there are certain difficulties involved in implementing what many call "sensitive content" into the curriculum. And Orlosky and Smith (1972), in discussing major changes affecting education during the past 75 years, point out the following:

A change that requires the teacher to abandon an existing practice and to displace it with a new practice risks defeat. If teachers must be retrained in order for a change to be made, as in team teaching, the chances of success are reduced unless strong incentives to be retrained are provided.[15]

The importance of teacher ownership and appropriate incentives cannot be minimized. Yet it is imperative that teachers be reeducated to enable them to face their responsibilities for making schools reflective of a pluralistic society. Only in this way can we eliminate the prevailing tendency among teachers to work with "more neutral and technical aspects of pedagogy."[16] Of primary importance for instituting multiculturalism into the school program are materials that help teachers to (a) develop self-awareness; (b) become knowledgeable about social and institutional norms; and (c) acquire an understanding of cultural, racial, sex, and individual differences. Addition-

---

[11]*Ibid.*, p. 31.

[12]Carl A. Grant and Susan L. Melnick. "Developing and Implementing Multicultural In-Service Teacher Education." Paper presented at the meeting of the National Council of States on In-Service Education. New Orleans, November 1976.

[13]Bruce R. Joyce, Kenneth R. Howey, and Sam J. Yarger. *ISTE, Report I: Issues to Face,* 1976.

[14]Dale Mann. "The Politics of Training Teachers in Schools." *Teachers College Record* 77: 326; 1976.

[15]Donald Orlosky and B. Othanel Smith. "Educational Change: Its Origins and Characteristics." *Phi Delta Kappan* 53: 414; March 1972.

[16]Dale Mann, "The Politics of Training Teachers in Schools," *op. cit.,* p. 326.

ally, teachers must utilize strategies of planned change and involvement in implementing proposed changes.

## Student Awareness Materials

Research on ethnic attitudes shows that children acquire prejudicial attitudes through parental and societal influences, often as early as the age of three or four. Goodman observes:

> By the age of four nearly all normal children will be at least minimally and occasionally aware of the physical marks of race and many will have developed distinct in-group/out-group *orientations* [incipient race attitudes].[17]

Rather than attempting to remedy thoroughly ingrained attitudes later in life, preventive strategies should be utilized early to inhibit the further development of negative attitudes toward people. By preventive strategies we mean the use of systematic strategies[18] (a) to help students develop a positive self-image, pride in and respect for their heritages and cultures, and (b) to help students develop an understanding of the nature and impact of racism, classism, and sexism. An understanding of these "terms" can be facilitated by using materials such as the film, *The Eye of the Storm*, which gave students in a third grade class in Nebraska insight into the nature and impact of prejudices by segregating them according to their blue and brown eye color. Students also need materials that will help them develop and apply critical thinking skills, which are necessary because biased instructional materials are used daily in our schools. Therefore, procedures and criteria for examining such biases are imperative. For example, students and teachers should develop a set of key questions to ask in relation to their instructional materials. Too frequently instructional materials are taken to be unquestioned authorities. Cronbach notes:

> Preparation of materials which will give pupils from the earliest grades a chance to *suspect* the word in print, without upsetting all their confidence in the school and without confusing them hopelessly, is an ideal worth suggesting to some teacher who would like to provide an innovation quite as dramatic as Comenius' or McGuffey's.[19]

An examination of primary reading textbooks over the past ten years

---

[17]Mary Ellen Goodman. *Race Awareness in Young Children.* New York: Anti-Defamation League, B'nai B'rith, 1964. p. 253.

[18]We purposely say "the use of systematic strategies" because the white middle-class social and instructional norms constantly operate as "hidden curricula" to make many minority and majority students feel inferior. Additionally, we do not think something as important as positive self-concept development should be left to chance.

[19]Lee J. Cronbach, *Text Materials in Modern Education, op. cit.,* p. 211.

reveals reasons that students need to be critical when using instructional materials.

In summary, some improvement is evident in the representation of cultural and racial minority groups and women in students' instructional materials, especially textbooks. However, textbooks today are still biased because (a) minority group individuals are still secondary characters in most integrated stories; (b) minority group characters are still too often described in stereotypic roles — for example, most stories that feature Native Americans represent them in terms of yesterday and not in the cultural realities of today; and (c) the number of stories with all minority group characters is very small.

## Classroom Materials

We believe that the implementation of multiculturalism demands both quality and quantity in classroom materials. Although teacher ownership requires that teachers be actively involved in the development and evaluation of classroom materials, we believe that some materials should be provided both as a model for teacher-made materials and to prevent slowing the implementation of multicultural education until teachers have time or adequate knowledge to develop their own. Thus, to eliminate the disadvantages of inadequate teacher preparation, lack of time, and uncertainty regarding appropriateness, materials should be developed by representatives of different cultures and racial groups to assure accuracy and be made readily available to teachers. Using these as a basis, teachers can begin to examine, develop, and evaluate other materials for use in their classrooms. The following criteria are recommended for examining the nature and content of classroom materials:

1. Reflect the pluralistic nature of our society as a positive feature of our nation's heritage and not present cultural, racial, and individual differences in isolation from each other.

2. Include a wide representation of the many cultures and races of the world and an equal representation of the cultures and races in the United States in all materials from kindergarten to twelfth grade.

3. Help students recognize and appreciate the contributions of culturally, racially, and individually different people to science, education, business and commerce, fine arts, communications, etc. In addition, contributions of diverse people in positions of authority should be recognized.

4. Present the cultural, racial, and individual differences among people in our society, using words and phrases that are complimentary and honest to build positive attitudes toward a student's own cultural and individual differences and acceptance of those of others.

5. Portray cultures other than from a "special occasion" point of view. For example: Are Native Americans presented mostly around Thanksgiving time? Is the study of blacks confined to Black History Week? Are Orientals usually studied around the time of the Chinese New Year?

Instead, examine real problems and real people, not just heroes and highlights, and portray culturally, racially, and individually different people as displaying various human emotions, both positive and negative.

6. Examine the social, economic, and political forces and conditions that optimize or minimize opportunities for individuals because of their race, culture, sex, age, or physical difference.

## Conclusion

Instructional materials will continue in the future, as they have in the past, to play a paramount role in the education of students and teachers. The knowledge gained can only be meaningful to our pluralistic society if the materials support the acceptance and affirmation of cultural, racial, sex, age, and physical differences.

# Applications

Multicultural activities should be integrated in all curriculum areas (social studies, language arts, science, etc.). The following Application section will provide the classroom teacher with ideas for activities they might use to illustrate the concept of multiculturalism as part of their classroom curriculum. These activities are suggestions. The creativity of the individual teacher will determine the extent and appropriateness of their use.

# 15

# Multicultural Activities for the Classroom Teacher

Mirian Ortiz and Lourdes Travieso

Multicultural education for today's society necessitates the development of new learning strategies and techniques to promote this concept within the classroom environment. Invalidation of the outdated "melting pot" theory that puts everyone into one cultural mold will only become possible with the realization that ours is a pluralistic society and that our strength lies in diversity itself.

Teachers must create an educational climate in which different cultural and linguistic patterns are accepted and nourished throughout the curriculum. Careful planning and direction are required to provide the necessary and appropriate experiences to capitalize on the child's cultural and linguistic resources. The classroom atmosphere must ensure the uniqueness of each child, and children should be encouraged to share their unique experiences with their peers.

Implementation of a multicultural setting which will permeate all facets of classroom life demands that sufficient time, effort, and energy be expended to this end. Teachers must be creative, flexible, sensitive and supportive, and must utilize all available resources, including the most valuable resources of all — their own students.

Teachers too often perceive the celebration of cultural holidays and/or the display of ethnic posters and "heroes" as the epitome of multicultural education. Unfortunately, these activities, valid as they may be, are not sufficient to create an understanding of the concepts of multiculturalism. They become "cliches" — taught in isolation, not integrated into the total curriculum design, and placed "back on the shelf" only to be dusted off and displayed the following year.

---

*Title:* **Music**.

*Concept:* A rich diversity of musical heritage is evident among people in different cultural groups and can be appreciated by all people throughout the world.

*Objectives:* To explore the many different types of music found throughout the world and the influences of diverse cultural backgrounds in creating this music.

To examine native and traditional instruments of cultural groups being studied.

*Grade level:* 4 — 12.

*Time:* Variable.

*Activities:* The teacher and students should discuss the value of music in their lives. How important is music to everyday life? What would it be like to go through a week without hearing music? The students should appreciate that music can be viewed as a "universal language," wherein one does not have to understand its intricacies in order to enjoy it.

Students should bring in and listen to folk records, songs, and dances representative of other countries and cultures. If available, perhaps a representative of a local record store could bring in and play some records from different cultures. Community members could also provide records for this purpose.

Following are but a few examples of topics for discussion that might arise after listening to music representative of other countries and cultures:

After listening to Caribbean music, try to distinguish the contributions and influences of the African, Indian, and Spanish cultures in the creation of unique musical pieces.

In a more modern blend, examine how Latin music and Black Rock have combined to create the new sound of "Salsa" (literal translation is sauce).

In the Chinese culture, such as that represented by the People's Republic of China, song and dance usually carry some kind of message. Some illustrative messages might be to defend our country, and to be healthy and strong.

Various national minorities, such as Tibetan, Mongolian, Korean, to mention a few, are represented in the Chinese culture. The Han culture is the dominant group. To reinforce the culturally pluralistic nature of the Chinese society, children learn to sing and dance the native folk music of the regions.

Also, the area of native and traditional instruments can provide a focus for many activities. These instruments can often be distinguished when listening to records representative of various cultures.

Students can research some of these instruments, for example, in Caribbean music you will find claves, guiros, maracas (Indian); congas, bongos (African); and guitars and cuatros (four doubled strings), (Spanish).

Traditional instruments in the Chinese culture are found in the cymbals, tambourine, flute, drums, sheng, erhu, liuchin, etc.

Students might find it interesting to research an instrument that is common to many different types of music to discover in which culture it originated. Another alternative would be to work in small groups on types of instruments, for example, percussion instruments or wind instruments.

Students could make their own instruments and try to develop their own unique musical sound.

*Title:* **Family**.

*Concept:* Teachers and the media, either directly or indirectly, often portray families in the United States as consisting of mother, father and children. Students, when faced with this image on a daily basis, might come to define the term "family" solely in this regard. However, an understanding that a particular term can have different meanings for different individuals is a prerequisite for meaningful communication in a pluralistic society.

*Objectives:* To enhance the self-respect of each child by focusing on different "possible" definitions for the term "family."

To provide an understanding that similarities and differences exist among and within families of different cultures.

To provide an understanding that family members can assume different roles, dependent upon the structure of the defined family unit.

*Grade level:* K — 2.

*Time:* Two weeks.

*Activities:* Before using the suggested activities to enhance this concept, the teacher must realize that many definitions for "family" will result from these activities. All reasonable definitions should be accepted; in essence, there are no right or wrong answers.

Students should discuss their families. Who are the members of their families? The teacher could write the names of each child's family on the board or the students can draw and label pictures of their families.

Possibilities that may be described by students:

Nuclear family (parents and children)
Extended family (including other family members)
Single-parent family (one parent)
Families without children (two adults)
No-parent family (child lives with another relative, with a guardian, or with another adult in a foster home).

Numerous cultures view their families in a broader perspective than the nuclear family. For example, the Hispanic culture embraces the concept of the extended family. This concept includes other adult members such as the "compadre" or "padrino" (literal translation is godfather). When Hispanic children are asked about the members of their families, they will probably include other adults with whom they have a very close kinship.

After students have finished listing or drawing the members of their families, prepare a wall mural. If a certain possibility has not surfaced because of the composition of your class, perhaps you could suggest and discuss this missing possibility.

Students should notice the different types of families that are illustrated on the wall mural. They will realize that many different types of families exist. Help them note similarities and differences among and within families of different cultures, that is, even though a particular culture embraces the concept of the extended family, some families within this culture may be nuclear families.

Students should derive their own definition of family, as a class, based upon their pictorial expressions.

Students should examine textbooks, magazines, newspapers, etc., to see what kinds of families can be found and what roles are played by individual family members. Students should realize that men, women, and children all can assume different roles, dependent upon the structure of the defined family unit. For example, does the man always head the family household?

Students can work on a booklet, "Families Can Be Many Different Things," or "Family Members Have Many Different Roles."

# 16

# Multicultural Activities for the Classroom

Gloria W. Grant

*Title:* **The Comics and Our Pluralistic Society.**

*Concept:* Since the comics speak a universal language of laughter, as well as depicting real life situations, all peoples should be equally represented in this media.

*Grade level:* K — 12.

*Time:* Teacher's discretion.

*Objective:* To discover the inclusion and the participation of all groups in the comics.

*Activities:* Students will bring to class the Sunday funnies from as many different newspapers as possible.

With younger children the teacher may wish to record the tallies with the class.

Working in teams of two, students will examine all of the comic strips and tally the race, sex, and age of persons and, if possible, the participation of persons as main or supporting characters, as well as the kinds of roles they play.

Students will share the results of their survey with the class and participate in a discussion with questions such as the following:

Who reads the comics?
Who is in the comics?
What are the characters doing?
Why are the comics mostly about white Americans?
Are there comics about other ethnic groups?
Who writes and illustrates the comics?

Students may want to pursue these questions further with local newspaper editors.

*Objective:* To create students' own multicultural comic strip. A multicultural comic strip should be balanced with male and female characters from all racial and cultural groups, the elderly and the handicapped. If balance is not possible with one comic strip, it should be evident throughout the total comic page. Roles characters play in each comic strip should not be stereotyped.[1]

*Activities:* Individually or in groups students will create their own comic strip. The strip may be written or dramatized. Color stereotyping of people should be avoided, for example, coloring Native Americans with a red crayon.

After the comic strip has been developed it should be evaluated for balance, stereotypes, roles and participation.

Students may wish to present this total project to other classes in the school or to local newspaper editors.

*Title:* **Changing Our View About the Elderly**

*Concept:* Since there are many stereotypes of the elderly in our society, it is important to provide students with the opportunity to develop a more positive attitude toward the elderly.

*Grade level:* K — 12

*Time:* Variable

*Objective:* To have students examine their perceptions about the elderly.

*Activities:* Students should be asked to define the word elderly and write it on the board.

A list should be made on the right side of the chalkboard of words that come into students' minds when they think of the elderly.

[1] See Carol Dodge's Chapter on Native Americans.

A list of reasons why students think the elderly have these assumed characteristics should also be recorded on chalkboard.

*Objective:* To have students become aware of the portrayal of the elderly in curriculum materials.

*Activities:* Students should examine textbooks and library books which feature the elderly.

On left side of chalkboard list words or phrases which describe the elderly found in textbooks or library books.

The lists should be compared and discussed for similarities and differences.

*Objective:* To have students expand perceptions of the elderly.

*Activities:* Elderly resource persons from different racial groups should be invited to the classroom. Students should plan questions they want to discuss. Older students may seek out elderly persons and interview them.

Descriptions, occupations, hobbies, etc. of the elderly from different racial groups should be discussed.

Students should, through individual research or by teacher direction, be exposed to stories and films which discuss the wide ranges of characteristics among the elderly.

Students should become aware of the accomplishments of the elderly from the teacher, learning center activity, bulletin board, individual research, and reports.

*Objective:* To have students reevaluate perceptions of the elderly.

*Activities:* Students will make a final list of words and phrases describing the elderly based on their own information.

The lists should then be compared with the original lists the class made.

Statements or stories by the class or individuals should be compiled to describe information learned about the elderly.

*Bulletin board idea:* A bulletin board idea on the elderly and their accomplishments would be to feature elderly people who have been working all their life and continue working into "old age," as well as those who have "just discovered" a talent in "old age".

*Title:* **Many Hands Made This Land**

*Concept:* Many people, regardless of their race, culture, age, sex, or physical handicap, have made significant contributions to the development of this country.

*Grade level:* K — 12, applicable to all subject areas.

*Time:* Ongoing.

*Objective:* To provide students with the opportunity to discover the accomplishments and the contributions of diverse people in the United States.

*Activities:* The classroom should have a bulletin board as a permanent part of the classroom which features, on a rotating basis, the accomplishments or contributions of diverse people.

The morning story or handwriting lesson for primary students should include information about diverse people.

Students should prepare oral reports elaborating on the contributions of diverse people. These reports may be shared with the class individually, in groups or in a panel discussion format.

Students should develop brief biographies of persons they have researched. These written reports may be used to develop a classroom library, and may be duplicated and given to each student to form a multicultural anthology.

*Instructional aids:* In order to facilitate this activity it is suggested that a list be made of possible categories, i.e., Art, Education, Entertainment, Journalism, Literature, Music, Politics, Science, and contributors within these categories.

*Title:* **The Handicapped Are Not "Really" Handicapped**

*Concept:* Handicapped people frequently are discriminated against because many people are not aware of their abilities. It is important for students to learn that many handicapped people hold responsible jobs in America's work force.

*Grade level:* 3 — 12

*Time:* Ongoing

*Objective:* To promote an understanding that handicapped people are a viable part of society's work force.

*Activities:* Students should contact the State Employment Office to ascertain the types of positions in which handicapped persons are employed and whether these positions are at the management or staff level.

Students should discuss the job performance of the handicapped with individuals who employ them. Questions should be raised regarding their attendance and the quality of their work.

*Objective:* To acknowledge the contributions of famous handicapped people.

*Activities:* Students should do library research on the varied contributions of famous handicapped persons — Thomas Edison, Franklin Delano Roosevelt, etc.

*Objective:* To become aware of the handicapped and their treatment in society.

*Activities:* Handicapped persons should visit the class and discuss their treatment by society in general and their reactions to this treatment.

---

*Title:* **How Much Have We Advanced Since Yesterday?**

*Concept:* Since many of the social, political, and economic issues of the past are still issues today, students should have an opportunity to become aware of these issues and the forces opposing their resolution.

*Grade level:* 6 — 12

*Time:* Several class periods for several weeks.

*Objective:* To compare and contrast the concerns of social leaders of the past with those of social leaders of today.

*Activities:* Students should read a speech delivered by or a book about a person from the past and a person from the present. Attention should also be paid to the social, political, or economic conditions of the time. Suggestions of characters are: Sojourner Truth, abolitionist; Barbara Jordan, U.S. House of Representatives; Chief Pontiac, Ottawa tribal chief; and Vine DeLoria, Jr., author.

*Objective:* To discover if the social conditions of the past have improved today, remained the same, or reversed.

*Activities:* Students should discuss in a role playing situation the concerns, perceptions, or dreams of the historical and contemporary persons. For example, what would Sojourner Truth say to Barbara Jordan today and vice versa?

*Objective:* To analyze forces in society that either hinder or promote improvement of the social conditions being discussed.

*Activities:* On opposite sides of paper or chalkboard, students should list forces in society which they feel either hinder or promote social conditions being discussed.

Students should discuss and list how opposing forces could be neutralized so that the social conditions in question could be improved.

# 17
# Cultural Traits

Anna Perez

---

*Title:* **Cultural Traits.**[1]

*Concept:* The appreciation and affirmation of diverse cultures in America are dependent upon an understanding of what culture is and how it is reflected in various traits.

*Objectives:* To aid students in understanding the meaning of culture.

To emphasize similarities and differences both among and within cultures.

To examine a variety of cultural traits.

To aid students in appreciating the importance of cultural maintenance.

*Grade level:* 3 — 12.

*Time:* One week.

*Activities:* A few days prior to a discussion of culture, the teacher will provide students access to a variety of materials illustrating the wide diversity of cultures in America. Suggestions for access include a new learning center, additions to a classroom library, a bulletin board, and/or visits to the IMC. Students should be encouraged to browse in their free time and to discuss their findings informally with their classmates.

---

[1]The basic idea for this activity comes from: *Nuestro Mundo Multietnico.* Fort Worth, Texas: Bilingual Materials Development Center, Department of Curriculum, 1976.

The teacher will initiate a discussion of culture with the total class or with small groups of students. Students should be encouraged to offer their own definitions or those which they have found in the materials they have examined. Although the precise wording of definitions may vary, the components of the following definitions from *Webster's New Collegiate Dictionary* (1976 edition) should be considered:

. . . the integrated pattern of human behavior that includes thought, speech, action, and artifacts and depends upon man's [sic] capacity for learning and transmitting knowledge to succeeding generations; . . . the customary beliefs, social forms, and material traits of a racial, religious, or social group.

General questions which might be used for discussion are as follows:

1. What is culture? . . . Tradition?
2. Are people born knowing how to act in ways acceptable to their culture? Why or why not?
3. What do people learn from others in their culture?

After discussing the various definitions offered by students, the class or groups should decide on one definition to be used as the basis of further discussion.

Have students divide into groups of 4 to 6. Using the definition previously decided upon, the teacher should assist students in describing the traits which reflect various cultures. Attention should be paid to languages, foods, clothes, customs, arts, ideas, the ways people act, what they believe in, their thoughts and feelings as individuals within a group. Since students may not be fully aware of the cultural implications of their daily behavior, it may be helpful to use an example such as the following:

Mexican American children know that when they enter a Mexican American home, they are to greet the adults with a handshake and "Buenos dias. Como esta?" or other appropriate words. This behavior is a cultural trait stemming from Mexican formality and respect for elders.

Students should make lists of cultural traits and their meanings within their groups. On the chalkboard or poster board, student recorders from each group should list the traits according to various cultures. The teacher should initiate a class discussion on the similarities and differences listed and on the significance of various traits.

Each student should select one culture to research in detail. Groups should be formed on the basis of student selections. The amount of time needed for research is left to teacher discretion. After completing the individual research activities, students should compare their findings with other students in their groups. A composite list should be prepared for sharing with the total class. Students should be encouraged to discuss similarities and differences among cultures based on their new-found information. Students should also examine their previous lists to be certain that all stereotypes have been removed.

The teacher should initiate discussion about the maintenance of cultural traits. General questions which might be used for discussion are as follows:

1. What is a "melting pot"?
2. Is the United States a melting pot? Why or why not?
3. What is meant by "assimilation"? What are the advantages or disadvantages of being assimilated?
4. Should one's cultural heritage be given up? Why or why not?
5. Who could or could not assimilate?

*Follow-up:* The above activities can serve as the introduction to a multicultural curriculum to be used throughout the school year. Immediate follow-up could include an art activity such as the following:

Have students construct a large wall mural illustrating cultural traits of diverse cultures. Students may complete the mural with drawings, words, and graffiti. Students may, for example, write "I Am Proud To Be a _____ Because _____," filling the blanks with their appropriate ethnic names or sex and reasons for their pride. To assure representation of all groups, students may complete the following: "Contributions Made by the _____ Include _____."

# 18

# Native Americans: Let's Eliminate the Stereotype

Carol Dodge

In this era of cultural pluralism, the American Indian is one of the most maligned of all groups. Most Americans have had no personal contact with Indians, and the limited familiarity they have with American Indian culture has come primarily from television or from books and classroom units on historical Indian life. Most textbooks portray the Indian population in a biased, negative manner and, as a result, detrimental stereotypes of Indians are still widely held. The following examples illustrate some of the most common stereotypes.

A major stereotype results from the tendency to generalize about all native people from Canada to South America as if they were members of one large tribe. The stereotypic portrayal usually focuses on a man on horseback, wearing a flowing feather bonnet, a breech cloth, and moccasins with a tomahawk in his hand. His wife is featured wearing a beaded brow-band with an upright feather at the back, a long beaded buckskin dress, and moccasins. The wife is usually shown with a papoose on her back, regardless of what she is doing, and the Indian family is shown living in a painted tipi. Generally, the husband carves totem poles, and the wife fashions painted pottery in her spare time. The elements included in this description can be found among *some* tribal groups in North America. But this symbolization is *not* an accurate description of all Indian tribes. As Stensland notes:

Whether [a teacher's] students are Indian or non-Indian, it is most important that the teacher recognize the vast diversity of Indian life styles and cultures. The Indian is not just Indian. [They] are Navajo or Sioux or Cherokee or Menominee or Micmac, etc. Which tribe [they] belong to or which combination of Indian backgrounds [they] come from makes all the difference in the way [they] think, [their] attitude toward life, and the kind of dress [they] put on for tribal celebrations.[1]

Another stereotypic concern is the prevalent distortion of Indian history and the almost total ignorance of contemporary Indian life. Development of Indian units is a major contributing factor in that the present tense is often used to describe the past. Or the teacher will end the unit after presenting a very romantic picture of Indian life, thus giving the illusion that modern Indian families live as their ancestors did 300 years ago, or, worse, that they vanished with Custer and the cavalry. Many of these units make comparisons that are out of context. For example, historical Indian life is compared or contrasted with contemporary non-Indian society, which often produces such a distorted image of the Indian people that Indian children don't even recognize themselves.

In all probability the most harmful stereotype results from the dominant society's tendency to present all of the Indians' faults and none of their virtues. This process of defamation condemns the Indian people to a status of inferiority in intelligence and adaptability. Consequently, most literature concerning both male and female leaders of the various tribes depicts them in degrading terms. If the biographies of the great chiefs, such as Joseph, Black Hawk, Tecumseh, Geronimo, Cochise, and Crazy Horse, for example, were written without the derogatory remarks, most people would realize that these leaders were men of religion and of peace who fought only to try to save their people and their lands. But the fighting, raiding, war-whooping Indian still dominates movies, television, textbooks, and many children's books. And words, such as "savage," "warlike," "crafty," and "shifty," which are especially demeaning to Indian children, are all too common.

The majority of curriculum materials about Indians have one common trait — superficial research as their basis. The following guidelines should be used by teachers to develop lesson plans or adapt existing materials:

1. Think of the Indian experience in terms of both contemporary and historical life. A historical perspective is useful, but failure to emphasize or even mention the current status of the American Indian constitutes a prejudicial portrayal. For example, a unit on traditional Indian life (the way they lived when Columbus arrived) should be contrasted with non-Indian life for that time period. Use the way the early settlers lived, rather than the way contemporary non-Indian society lives.

2. When teaching a unit on traditional Indian life, bring it up-to-date as you do the non-Indian culture, instead of leaving Indians living in the past.

---

[1]Anna Lee Stensland. *Literature by and about the American Indian.* Urbana, Illinois: National Council of Teachers of English, 1973. p. 15. Copyright © 1973 by the National Council of Teachers of English. Reprinted with permission.

3. Activities on Indians should be realistic, informative, and without deception, regardless of the ages of the students. Accuracy can be achieved only through adequate research. In other words, don't rely on Squanto, Pocahontas, and Sacajawea. They became famous because of their friendship with the Europeans, and not because of what they did for the Indian people.

4. Most important, teachers should design lessons which study tribal groups by region, especially emphasizing those in one's own area. If you live in Wisconsin, for example, study the tribes residing in the state, and then compare them with those living in the Southwest. Care should be taken in the use of visual aids, books, etc., which claim to represent the tribes in your area but are actually characteristic of tribes located in distant parts of the country. For example, when studying Menominees, a woodland tribe, visual aids illustrating the tipi, the war bonnet, and the horse with travoise, although perhaps easily accessible, are inappropriate because these items are characteristic of Plains Indians.

5. Lastly, teachers must enter into the units with the same open minds they expect of students. It is important for teachers to think in terms of new learning experiences, not only for their students, but for themselves as well.

In keeping with the foregoing guidelines, the following are offered as possible topics from which teachers can develop classroom activities that portray contemporary American Indian life honestly and accurately.

1. With the use of maps have students identify contemporary reservation areas.[2] These may be compared with reservation areas from the past.

2. Have students write to the Area Directors of Bureau of Indian Affairs field offices[3] for information on tribes under their jurisdiction. They may wish to ask questions regarding the following:

a. The size and description of reservations.

b. Population and names of tribes located on reservation. (The name of reservation doesn't always indicate what tribe(s) is located there. For example, Wind River Reservation, Wyoming, is the home of both the Eastern Shoshoni and Northern Arapahoe.)

c. What are the natural resources? (Keep in mind that when the tribes were placed on the reservations, the lands were considered sub-marginal and areas that no one else wanted. Now they are finding valuable minerals on several of these reservations. What effect do you think this has on the tribal groups living there? Who decides what happens to the minerals?)

[2]Maps may be secured from the following sources: "3 Maps of Indian Country," Publication Service, Haskell Indian Jr. College, Lawrence, Kansas 66044; "Indian Land Areas," (Stock # 2402-0025), Superintendent of Documents, U.S. Government Printing Office, Washington, D.C. 20402; "American Indian Tribes Map," (Stock # I-1283-430), Southwest Book Service, 2200 N. Scottsdale Road, Scottsdale Plaza, Scottsdale, Arizona 85257.

[3]Names can be secured from the Bureau of Indian Affairs, Washington, D.C.

3. Sometimes the Department of the Interior reclaims land for such things as dams, tourist areas, etc. Have students research when and where this has happened. How much land was flooded? What happened to the tribes living in the area? How was their consent obtained to give up the land?

4. Have students visually describe an "Indian" or "Indians" by making collages. Have students examine the collages for possible stereotypes. Discuss with them whether they would recognize an Indian on TV, in the movies, or in a book or magazine, without all the buckskin and feathers. (What are the implications?)

5. Look through the IMC or library for audiovisual materials about American Indians. Have students compare examples of historical vs. contemporary life. You will probably find a dearth of material on contemporary Indians. Discuss with students why most material is historical in nature. What implications does this have for giving wrong impressions of Indians?

6. Have older students evaluate children's books about Indians, especially those dealing with pioneer life. Discuss what part these books play in continuing stereotypes.

# Authors

*Michael W. Apple* is a Professor of Curriculum and Instruction at the University of Wisconsin, Madison. He has been active in the student rights movement. He has also served as a child and parent advocate and as a consultant in legal cases involving the rights of politically active educators. Among his recent publications are *Educational Evaluation: Analysis and Responsibility* and *Schooling and the Rights of Children*.

*H. Prentice Baptiste, Jr.,* is Chairperson of the Multicultural/Bilingual Education Program Area at the University of Houston, where he developed the University's first doctoral program in multicultural education. He has written articles, developed media presentations, and served as consultant on the education of black children, on science education, and on multicultural education. He is currently co-editing a book of readings in multicultural education that will include his article on the future of the field.

141

*Mira Baptiste* has taught in public schools at the elementary and secondary levels, has been a school district supervisor for the Title I reading program, and is currently a principal in the Houston Independent School System. She has worked extensively in teacher training and curriculum development at the University of Houston, served as consultant on multicultural education, and conducted in-service workshops in Texas, Oregon, and Missouri.

A member of the Executive Staff of the National Council for the Social Studies, *Mary F. Crum* shares the responsibility for the planning and implementation of the organization's national and regional programs and is directly responsible for the Council's information and referral services. She recently edited a Bibliography on Teacher Centers in America for the ERIC Clearinghouse on Teacher Education, and coordinated the reports and publications for the 1976 Bicentennial National Education Week Program.

*Carol Dodge* is a Menominee Indian who lives on the Menominee Indian Reservation in Wisconsin. She is the Curriculum Coordinator for the Menominee Indian School District.

*Geneva Gay* is Associate Director of the Association for Supervision and Curriculum Development. She has been a high school social studies teacher, an Assistant Professor of Curriculum and Instruction at the University of Texas, and Acting Chairperson of Afro-American Studies at the University of Texas, Austin. She is the author of several articles, and has served as consultant to school districts, colleges and professional associations in the areas of ethnic and cultural diversity and multicultural education.

*Carl A. Grant* is Assistant Professor of Education at the University of Wisconsin-Madison and Director of the Teacher Corps Associates Program. He is currently engaged in research in the area of teacher role expectations and the implementation of education that is multicultural in a school setting. His most recent books are *Community Participation in Education* (1977), and *In Praise of Diversity: A Resource Book for Multicultural Education* (with Rivlin and Gold). He is Chairperson of the ASCD Multicultural Commission.

*Gloria W. Grant* has written numerous articles in the area of multicultural education. She is nationally known for her workshops on the evaluation of instruction materials. Her most recent publication is *In Praise of Diversity: Multicultural Classroom Applications* (1977).

*James B. Macdonald* is Distinguished Professor of Education at the University of North Carolina-Greensboro. He was formerly head of the Department of Curriculum at the University of Wisconsin, and has published extensively in the field of curriculum. He has taught at the University of London, the University of Texas, and New York University. While serving on the ASCD Executive Council he was elected to represent that body as a member of the Multicultural Commission in 1975-76.

*Susan L. Melnick* has written a number of articles and has conducted workshops on language programs for the linguistically different, Education that is Multicultural, inservice education, and bilingual methods and materials. She is currently a Research and Teaching Assistant in the Department of Curriculum and Instruction, University of Wisconsin-Madison, where she is completing her Ph.D. dissertation on the language of teacher role expectations.

*William M. Newman* (M.A., Syracuse University, Ph.D., New School for Social Research) is Associate Professor of Sociology at the University of Connecticut. He is the author of *American Pluralism* (1973) and the editor of *The Social Meanings of Religion* (1974). He is presently serving as a contributing editor to the *Review of Religious Research* and is general editor of the Society for the Scientific Study of Religion Monograph Series. His primary areas of teachings and research are intergroup relations, sociology of religion, and social theory.

*Mirian Ortiz* is the Team Leader of the Bilingual Teacher Corps program at P.S. 192-M in New York. She has taught on the elementary level and at the City College of New York. She is presently a member of the Teacher Corps Associates Program at the University of Wisconsin in Madison.

*Anna Louise Valdez Perez* grew up in the southside barrio of Fort Worth, Texas and received her education in the public schools. She has a bachelor's degree in elementary education, and a master's degree in special education from Texas Christian University in Fort Worth, Texas. She has taught in the Fort Worth Independent School District's bilingual education, human relations, and special education programs. For the past two years, she has been the Team Leader with the Texas Christian University/Fort Worth Independent School District Teacher Corps Project.

*Muriel Saville-Troike* has degrees in English, education, and linguistics, and has had teaching experience ranging from kindergarten to university levels. She is a Past President of Teachers of English to Speakers of Other Languages (TESOL) and author of numerous publications in applied linguistics, including *Foundations for Teaching English as a Second Language: Theory and Method in Multicultural Education* (1976), and *A Handbook of Bilingual Education* (1971).

*Allen A. Schmieder* is Chief of Support Programs for the Division of Educational Systems Development in the United States Office of Education and Program Director of the National Teacher Center Program. A notable publication relative to the subject of this book was his base paper for the 1977 United Nations International Congress on Environmental Education, *The Nature and Philosophy of (International) Environmental Education: Some Fundamental Goals, Concepts, Objectives and Developmental Issues.*

*William L. Smith* is Director of the Teacher Corps, U.S. Office of Education. He has been a teacher, guidance counselor, and school principal, and has extensive international experience in education, having served as a U.S. Delegate to educational projects in Western Europe and as guest lecturer for the Polish Ministry of Education. He has written numerous articles on teacher education, urban and black education, and multicultural education.

*Lourdes Travieso* is the Director of the Bilingual Teacher Corps program for the New York City School District, Center for Bilingual Education, and the City College of New York. A former National Urban Fellow, sponsored by the Ford Foundation and Yale University, she has written and spoken extensively on the bilingual/bicultural child and was recently a member of the U.S.O.E. National Task Force on Instructional Strategies in Schools with High Concentrations of Low-Income Pupils.

*Kaoru Yamamoto* is currently Professor of Education at Arizona State University. He has been interested in the exploration of developmental processes, mental health in education, and humane inquiry into human affairs. His publications include *Individuality* (1975) and *Death in the Life of Children* (1977). He is a Fellow of the American Psychological Association, and the immediate past editor of the *American Educational Research Journal.*

*Florence Makita Yoshiwara* is President and former Co-ordinator of the Japanese American Curriculum Project, Inc., in San Mateo, California. As a Title IV Advisory Specialist for the San Mateo City School District she worked in curriculum development for human relations and multi-cultural education with emphasis on what it means to be a Japanese American. She has written textbooks, articles, and audiovisual presentations on multiculturalism and on the Japanese American experience.

# Acknowledgments

Final editing of the manuscript and publication of this yearbook were the responsibility of Robert R. Leeper, Associate Director and Editor, ASCD publications. Production was handled by Elsa Angell with the assistance of Patsy Connors, Teola T. Jones, and Myra Taub, with Nancy Olson as production manager. The cover and design of this volume are by Linda S. Sherman.

# ASCD Publications, Summer 1977

## Yearbooks

Balance in the Curriculum (610-17274) — $5.00
Education for an Open Society (610-74012) — $8.00
Education for Peace: Focus on Mankind (610-17946) — $7.50
Evaluation as Feedback and Guide (610-17700) — $6.50
Feeling, Valuing, and the Art of Growing: Insights into the Affective (610-77104) — $9.75
Freedom, Bureaucracy, & Schooling (610-17508) — $6.50
Leadership for Improving Instruction (610-17454) — $4.00
Learning and Mental Health in the School (610-17674) — $5.00
Life Skills in School and Society (610-17786) — $5.50
A New Look at Progressive Education (610-17812) — $8.00
Perspectives on Curriculum Development 1776-1976 (610-76078) — $9.50
Schools in Search of Meaning (610-75044) — $8.50
Perceiving, Behaving, Becoming: A New Focus for Education (610-17278) — $5.00
To Nurture Humaneness: Commitment for the '70's (610-17810) — $6.00

## Books and Booklets

Action Learning: Student Community Service Projects (611-74018) — $2.50
Adventuring, Mastering, Associating: New Strategies for Teaching Children (611-76080) — $5.00
Beyond Jencks: The Myth of Equal Schooling (611-17928) — $2.00
The Changing Curriculum: Mathematics (611-17724) — $2.00
Criteria for Theories of Instruction (611-17756) — $2.00
Curricular Concerns in a Revolutionary Era (611-17852) — $6.00
Curriculum Leaders: Improving Their Influence (611-76084) — $4.00
Curriculum Materials 1974 (611-74014) — $2.00
Degrading the Grading Myths: A Primer of Alternatives to Grades and Marks (611-76082) — $6.00
Differentiated Staffing (611-17924) — $3.50
Discipline for Today's Children and Youth (611-17314) — $1.50
Early Childhood Education Today (611-17766) — $2.00
Educational Accountability: Beyond Behavioral Objectives (611-17856) — $2.50
Elementary School Mathematics: A Guide to Current Research (611-75056) — $5.00
Elementary School Science: A Guide to Current Research (611-17726) — $2.25
Eliminating Ethnic Bias in Instructional Materials: Comment and Bibliography (611-74020) — $3.25
Emerging Moral Dimensions in Society: Implications for Schooling (611-75052) — $3.75

Ethnic Modification of Curriculum (611-17832) — $1.00
Global Studies: Problems and Promises for Elementary Teachers (611-76086) — $4.50
The Humanities and the Curriculum (611-17708) — $2.00
Humanizing the Secondary School (611-17780) — $2.75
Impact of Decentralization on Curriculum: Selected Viewpoints (611-75050) — $3.75
Improving Educational Assessment & An Inventory of Measures of Affective Behavior (611-17804) — $4.50
International Dimension of Education (611-17816) — $2.25
Interpreting Language Arts Research for the Teacher (611-17846) — $4.00
Learning More About Learning (611-17310) — $2.00
Linguistics and the Classroom Teacher (611-17720) — $2.75
A Man for Tomorrow's World (611-17838) — $2.25
Middle School in the Making (611-74024) — $5.00
The Middle School We Need (611-75060) — $2.50
Multicultural Education: Commitments, Issues, and Applications (611-77108) — $7.00
Needs Assessment: A Focus for Curriculum Development (611-75048) — $4.00
Observational Methods in the Classroom (611-17948) — $3.50
Open Education: Critique and Assessment (611-75054) — $4.75
Open Schools for Children (611-17916) — $3.75
Personalized Supervision (611-17680) — $1.75
Professional Supervision for Professional Teachers (611-75046) — $4.50
Removing Barriers to Humaneness in the High School (611-17848) — $2.50
Reschooling Society: A Conceptual Model (611-17950) — $2.00
The School of the Future—NOW (611-17920) — $3.75
Schools Become Accountable: A PACT Approach (611-74016) — $3.50
Social Studies for the Evolving Individual (611-17952) — $3.00
Staff Development: Staff Liberation (611-77106) — $6.50
Supervision: Emerging Profession (611-17796) — $5.00
Supervision in a New Key (611-17926) — $2.50
Supervision: Perspectives and Propositions (611-17732) — $2.00
The Unstudied Curriculum: Its Impact on Children (611-17820) — $2.75
What Are the Sources of the Curriculum? (611-17522) — $1.50
Vitalizing the High School (611-74026) — $3.50
Developmental Characteristics of Children and Youth (wall chart) (611-75058) — $2.00

Discounts on quantity orders of same title to single address: 10-49 copies, 10%; 50 or more copies, 15%. Make checks or money orders payable to ASCD. Orders totaling $10.00 or less must be prepaid. Orders from institutions and businesses must be on official purchase order form. Shipping and handling charges will be added to billed purchase orders. **Please be sure to list the stock number of each publication, shown in parentheses.**

Subscription to **Educational Leadership**—$10.00 a year. ASCD Membership dues: Regular (subscription and yearbook)—$25.00 a year; Comprehensive (includes subscription and yearbook plus other books and booklets distributed during period of membership)—$35.00 a year.

Order from: **Association for Supervision and Curriculum Development Suite 1100, 1701 K Street, N.W., Washington, D.C. 20006**